arts
with
the
brain
in
mind

Eric Jensen

**Association for Supervision
and Curriculum Development**

Alexandria, Virginia USA

Association for Supervision and Curriculum Development
1703 N. Beauregard St. · Alexandria, VA 22311-1714 USA
Telephone: 1-800-933-2723 or 703-578-9600 · Fax: 703-575-5400
Web site: http://www.ascd.org · E-mail: member@ascd.org

Illustrations by Eric Jensen.

Note: There was no financial support or any other potential conflict of interest from any of the many fine organizations that commonly support the arts.

ASCD publications present a variety of viewpoints. The views expressed or implied in this book should not be interpreted as official positions of the Association.

Printed in the United States of America.

May 2001 member book (p). ASCD Premium, Comprehensive, and Regular members periodi-cally receive ASCD books as part of their membership benefits. No. FY01-07.

ASCD Product No. 101011
ASCD member price: $18.95   nonmember price: $22.95

Library of Congress Cataloging-in-Publication Data
Jensen, Eric.
  Arts with the brain in mind/Eric Jensen.
    p. cm.
Includes bibliographical references and index.
"ASCD product no. 101011 " --T.p. verso.
 ISBN 0-87120-514-9 (alk. paper)
 1. Arts--Study and teaching--United States. 2. Cognition in children--United States. 3. Curriculum planning--United States. I Title.
  LB1591.5.U57 J46 2001
  700'.71 '273--dc21
                        2001000735

07 06 05 04 03   10 9 8 7 6 5 4 3 2

Arts with the Brain in Mind

Acknowledgments

To dedicated neuroscientists Lawrence Parsons, V. S. Ramachandran, Gordon Shaw, and Norman Weinberger.

Many thanks to the incomparable MUSICA newsletter (http://www.musica.uci.edu).

To the countless arts advocates who are making a difference every day.

To Don Campbell, who planted the seeds in my brain to write the book.

To Bob Sylwester, who inspired me to think about the topic in a novel way.

To jazz pianist Harry Pickens, whose music has brought joy to my soul.

To my researcher extraordinaire Rick Crowley.

To a patient Mark Goldberg, the editor who always believes in my next book.

Preface

I think it's fair for me to state up front what my biases are. You deserve to know what flavors this book. First, I am not, in any traditional way, an artist. We all create our lives in a broadly artistic way, and writing is certainly some kind of art or skill. But I have no vested interest in pushing any particular art expression. Second, I have no children enrolled in any schools where I'm trying to influence someone's education, in particular. And third, I am deeply committed to making a significant, positive, and lasting contribution to the education of all children. Although I do workshops and speak at conferences on learning with the brain in mind, I am, above all, an *advocate for improving education*. It has been through my research that I have come to support the arts.

This book is an exploration of how I came to support the arts. I started with three major questions. First, how do the arts stack up as a major discipline? Second, what is their effect on the brain, learning, and human development? Third, how might schools best implement and assess an arts program?

Education is not an either-or scenario. It's not the arts versus a rigorous, demanding curriculum. I want learning to be engaging, challenging, vigorous, and integrated. The arts should not be a path only for the alternative learner or those who would otherwise fail, any more than math is an easy path for those who can't do arts. I favor challenging work in all the disciplines (arts as one of them), with regular, accurate, and purposeful assessment and strong standards in learning.

Education must be attentive to individual differences and community building. Student-centered learning is better than teacher-centered learning. I support constructivism over mindless factual accumulation, and I favor depth over breadth of knowledge. I favor variety in education over one-size-fits-all. I want our schools to foster ethical, fair-minded, disciplined, cooperative, thoughtful, considerate, problem-solving, creative citizens.

Flying in the face of these hopes is an educational juggernaut unlike any we've seen in recent history. It's called "higher standards," and it's the latest version of the politician's Holy Grail. Some believe that higher standards will ensure that all learners do better in school. That may or may not be true. But there is no evidence that higher standards actually produces better human beings—unless accompanied by better-quality teaching, more targeted resources, greater opportunities for underserved populations, stronger role models, high expectations, and a dozen other key variables.

To reach these standards, educators seek some kind of strategy to get over the hump—some kind of "magic pill." Some are calling for a more rigorous core curriculum; for others, it's learning styles; and still others are determined that the multiple intelligences model will do the trick. The fact is, humans are unique; and educators need different approaches and strategies to reach a wide range of learners. Believe it or not, many schools, districts, and states have been using a powerful solution for decades. It's called the arts.

By making arts a core part of the basic curriculum and thoughtfully integrating the arts into every subject, you might not get the high test scores you want immediately. The evidence is mixed on that issue, though it leans in favor of the arts. If you do get higher scores, it certainly won't happen overnight. But much more important, you may get fewer dropouts, higher attendance, better team players, an increased love of learning, greater student dignity, enhanced creativity, a more prepared citizen for the workplace of tomorrow, and greater cultural awareness as a bonus. This book demonstrates that the collective data not only support the value of widespread arts implementation, but the evidence also shows no downside risk.

Only 28 of 50 states in the United States have arts requirements for graduation (Kantrowitz & Leslie, 1997). At least, that's up from just 2 states in 1980. A federally mandated basic arts education policy does not exist. That's not just embarrassing and inexcusable; it's irresponsible. Sufficient data exist to overwhelmingly support the fundamental value and role of arts on equal standing with every other so-called academic discipline, including science, languages, and math. It can no longer be called a "cultural add-on" or "right-brained frill." The times are changing, and arts are roaring back into curriculums with renewed purpose. They can no longer be targeted as a desperate solution for inner-city schools.

Art advocates are constantly being asked to show evidence that, for example, music improves math scores. Let's turn that around: Does math improve music? No one asks the questions, "Does math improve the arts? Does science improve reading? Does English actually improve the mind, or does it only serve as an accumulation of a snobbish bravado?" The fact is, we have historically assumed that other disciplines (excluding art) are valuable; yet they are not held to the same level of scrutiny to which art is now being held. For the few who remain convinced, after reading this book, that the arts are a frill, you might as well let computers take over and run civilization from a motherboard in an underground silo. Without arts, we can pack our tents, admit we have lost our humanity, and all go home to an online, pay-per-grade, computer-based education.

As we begin the new millennium, one of the questions raised will be "What can't technology do?" Computers will amass, modify, and manipulate data like never before. Revolutionary software programs will calculate, sort, summarize, write, edit, translate, compose, and present knowledge in unimaginable new ways. But what makes us most human is what will be the most desirable commodity. That's the ability to thoughtfully regulate, express, and channel emotions into arts such as music, performances, movement, painting, and design. Art will increase, not decrease in value.

The thesis of this book is that arts are not only fundamental to success in our demanding, highly technical, fast-moving world, but they are what makes us most human, most complete as people. Arts contribute to our growth as human beings. The time has come to take the arts seriously. At a time when higher standards are being thrust on all of us, arts have an even bigger place. Even if one *could* get the higher scores without a basic or integrated arts curriculum, do you really want to live in a world where the best that we have to offer is a high-test-score graduate, but a person who can't work with others, be creative and express himself, solve real-world problems, and do it with civility? I would not choose that world; would you?

Obviously, I'm making some strong claims about the value of arts. I want you to know I did not come to that decision frivolously. In this book I cite the scientific basis for my claims, as well as provide real-world examples of how to implement and how to assess an arts program. Though there will still be skeptics who are uncomfortable with a stronger arts role in school, the facts are in: You can make as good a case, or better, for arts than you can make for any other discipline.

1 The *Arts* as a Major Discipline

*R*ight from the start, it's imperative to understand that evidence from brain research is *only one* of many reasons to support the arts as an integral part of the educational process. There are studies that report benefits from a long-term arts curriculum, but many of them are deficient in some respect (Eisner, 1998). A recent Project Zero study (2000) cautioned against making causal links between arts and academic performance. This Harvard group is correct; arts are not to be used as a "quick fix" to shore up other nagging deficits in a district's educational process. Arts are for the long term; and one should be cautious in claims about how they affect test scores. In fact, a report by the Arts Education Partnership and the President's Committee on the Arts and the Humanities, funded by General Electric Corporation and the John D. and Catherine T. MacArthur Foundation, *Champions of Change* (Fiske, 1999), suggests that the influence of the arts is far wider and deeper than simply improved letter grades.

If we place value only on higher test scores—and if the tests measure only math, problem-solving, and verbal skills—the arts are at a clear disadvantage. If we demand quick results, the arts will not supply them. The arts develop neural systems that often take months and years to fine-tune. The benefits, when they appear, will be sprinkled across the spectrum, from fine motor skills to creativity and improved emotional balance.

In today's educational climate, delaying returns on investment beyond a few weeks is considered inefficient and sinful; and since art-making is inefficient, how does one justify arts in the curriculum? In the past, supporters of arts education tried to show it boosted test scores in other disciplines. Judith Burton of Columbia University gathered research to show that subjects such as science, mathematics, and language require complex cognitive and creative capacities "typical of arts learning" (Burton, Horowitz, & Abeles, 1999).

Eventually, though, the way the question is framed changes to, "Does music help math?" "Does art help language?" "Does P.E. help science?" That is ludicrous. The arts do not need—and may not be able—to justify their existence that way.

Second, and paradoxically, *even if* the arts did help every other discipline to a degree, it may not be the most efficient way to learn them. If students learn history through the arts, couldn't they learn it faster by doing it much more directly? It's essential to recognize that in this recent push for greater school efficiency (e.g., every minute counts), the arts are terribly inefficient. It is dreadfully time consuming to learn visual, musical, and movement arts. A theater group might rehearse for 100 minutes a day for 100 days to put on a single 90-minute play. For other students, long hours over several years are invested, with marginal artistic results. So now the question shifts to, If arts are not efficient, what are they?

Art as a Brain Developer

The central theme of this book is that the arts promote the development of valuable human neurobiological systems. Theories of the brain exist that help us understand what is going on when we do art. Chapters 2–4 introduce separate theories for the musical, visual, and kinesthetic arts. It's not enough to say that the arts *probably* benefit us; we ought to be able to articulate what goes on in the brain to make that happen. Chapter 5 addresses controversial arts assessment issues.

The arts enhance the process of learning. The systems they nourish, which include our integrated sensory, attentional, cognitive, emotional, and motor capacities, are, in fact, the driving forces behind all other learning. That doesn't mean that one cannot learn without the arts; many have. The arts, however, provide learners with opportunities to simultaneously develop and mature multiple brain systems, none of which are easy to assess because they support processes that yield cumulative results. The systems and *processes* are not, in and of themselves, *the results*. Testing the processes instead of results can narrow the development of the very neurobiological systems they depend on. Students will restrict their artistic activities in hopes of better grades.

It may be more important, finally, to value the nonacademic benefits of the arts. Why be sheepish about the possibility that the arts may promote self-discipline and motivation? What's embarrassing about countless *other* art benefits that include aesthetic awareness, cultural exposure, social harmony, creativity, improved emotional expression, and appreciation of diversity? Aren't these the underpinnings of a healthy culture? In *Champions of Change: The Impact of the Arts* on Learning, the contributors highlight some of the "take-home" messages about arts (Fiske, 1999):

· The arts reach students not ordinarily reached, in ways not normally used. This keeps tardies and truancies and, eventually, dropouts down.

· Students connect to each other better—greater camaraderie, fewer fights, less racism, and reduced use of hurtful sarcasm.

· It changes the environment to one of discovery. This can re-ignite the love of learning in students tired of being filled up with facts.

· Arts provide challenges for students at all levels, from delayed to gifted. It's a class where all students can find their own level, automatically.

· Arts connect learners to the world of real work where theater, music, and products have to appeal to a growing consumer public.

· Students learn to become sustained, self-directed learners, not a repository of facts from direct instruction for the next high-stakes test

· Students of lower socioeconomic status gain as much or more from arts instruction than those of higher socioeconomic status. This suggests the gifted programs need to expand their target audiences.

So the arts should be taught not only because there is some science that argues for their inclusion. We should support the arts in education because of their dynamic and broad-based value as a peer of every other widely accepted discipline.

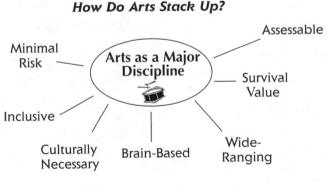

How Do Arts Stack Up?

Arts as a Major Discipline

Minimal Risk · Assessable · Survival Value · Inclusive · Culturally Necessary · Brain-Based · Wide-Ranging

What Makes a Major Discipline?

Let's start with a question. What makes a subject or discipline a "major discipline"? How do we decide what is worth making everybody study and learn? It's a difficult question, well worth exploring. I believe educators can use seven criteria to define major disciplines like science or languages. Let's discover whether or not the arts receive a passing grade as a major discipline.

1. Is the discipline assessable? Assessing the arts can and has been done. In Wisconsin, a coalition of art educators has worked closely with state leaders to create a comprehensive quality arts assessment (e.g., Wisconsin Department of Public Instruction, 1997). *Whether* the arts should be assessed is a topic we'll explore later. For testing purposes, the arts are often broken down into the visual, musical, and kinesthetic (or movement) arts. But there are other ways to organize them. Many organizations, districts, and committees have done admirable, and at times, stunning jobs developing measurable criteria for excellence in all of the arts. Chapter 5 addresses the assessment issue in detail. **Grade for the arts: Pass.**

2. Is it brain based? Here we ask if there's a built-in biological basis for the discipline. Is it hard-wired into the brain? Are there identifiable places in the brain that respond only to that discipline? After all, there are language centers in the brain—what about the arts? As it happens, brain research in each of the three subdisciplines—visual, musical, and kinesthetic—has located anatomical structures dedicated to processing specific art experiences. Back in the late '70s and early '80s a myth arose that the arts are just a right-brain frill. This hang-over from the days of the "left brain is logical and the right brain is creative" is dead wrong. Chapters 2–4 present brain-based evidence showing the biological basis for art-making. And not only do the arts engage many areas of the brain (see Figure 1.1), but they also have multiple, far-reaching effects on the learner's mind. This book presents a comprehensive arts-based brain theory. **Grade for the arts: Pass.**

3. Is it culturally necessary? A discipline should serve clear cultural needs. It should promote the betterment of humanity as well as of local culture. In disciplines such as science the answer to this question is obvious. Learn science, then invent a vaccine like for polio and you're Jonas Salk. But what about the arts? Do they serve clear needs? The answer is yes. The arts promote the understanding and sharing of culture. The arts promote social skills that enhance awareness of others and tolerance of differences. The arts promote unity and harmony. They enhance cognitive and perceptual skills. They serve as vehicles for cultural identity and free expression. At Columbia University, Judith Burton's study of more than 2,000 children found that those in an arts curriculum were far superior in creative thinking, self-concept, problem-solving, self-expression, risk-taking, and cooperation than those who were not (Burton et al., 1999). **Grade for the arts: Pass.**

4. What is the downside risk? There must be a minimal or zero downside to education in the discipline. Could it hamper the learning process? Does it impede the learning of other disciplines—or potentially harm a person? There are no known cases where an arts curriculum, either integrated or modular, has, by itself, lowered test scores, increased problems, or reduced graduation rates. Even when the teaching of art is done at a suboptimal level, learners derive some benefit. **Grade for the arts: Pass.**

5. Is the discipline inclusive? A major discipline cannot be elitist. Can it be learned, if not mastered, by an overwhelming majority of students? Research and our own experience show that all levels of society can and do participate in the arts. Race, religion, culture, geography, and socioeconomic levels do not constitute barriers. In fact, underserved populations receive more benefit from exposure to the arts than other children. In the landmark document *Champions of Change,* Catterall, Chapleau, and Iwanaga (1999) report that 21 percent of students of low socioeconomic status who had been exposed to music scored high in math versus just 11 percent of those who had not. By 12th grade, the figures grew to 33 percent and 16 percent, respectively, suggesting a cumulative value to music education. The Suzuki method is another demonstration that nearly everyone can become a competent musician. The arts have the capacity to engage us all. **Grade for the arts: Pass.**

6. Does it have survival value? Is this discipline necessary for the species to survive? Mastering the skills of language or scientific inquiry clearly enhances survival. You can succeed in—not just cope with—this fast-moving world. The arts help, too, in less self-evident ways. Communities survive based not only on their technology, but also their culture. Art creates, enhances, and defines culture. The work of two cultural anthropologists (Coe, 1990; Dissayanake, 1988) demonstrates that art-making has been present for thousands of years, and may guide survival. Art-making facilitates the creation of large, strong communities that embody important values. These community values are established and shared through the metaphors of the visual, musical, and kinesthetic arts. **Grade for the arts: Pass.**

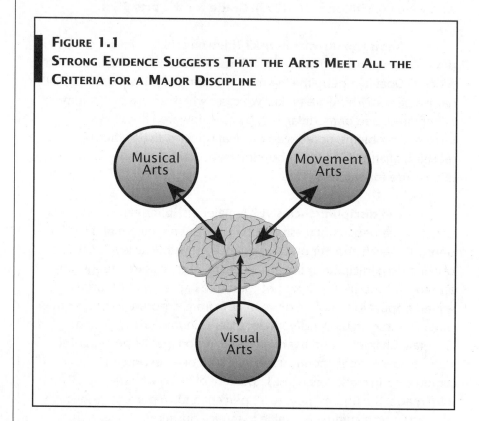

FIGURE 1.1
STRONG EVIDENCE SUGGESTS THAT THE ARTS MEET ALL THE CRITERIA FOR A MAJOR DISCIPLINE

7. Is it wide ranging? The discipline must have subdisciplines that add breadth, depth, and credibility. We all recognize the tremendous breadth and depth of disciplines such as science, from biology to chemistry, from physics to electronics. The arts can hold their head just as high. Among the musical arts, we can include performance, listening, composing, arranging, analysis, singing, improvisation, and song writing. In the visual arts we can list drawing, photography, decoupage, illustration, costume design, computer-based graphics, film-making, set design, and the creation of communication tools. In the movement arts, the ranges run from physical education through drama, games, improvisation, dance, auto mechanics, sports, crafting, stretching or aerobic fitness, as well as disciplines like martial arts, yoga, and Tai Chi. Taken as a whole, the arts are wide ranging and deep in substance. **Grade for the arts: Pass.**

The arts should not be held to more rigorous standards than other major disciplines. Nor should they be held to any less of a standard. The criteria we've examined show the arts as fit for inclusion in the curriculum as any other discipline. Not just sometimes, when you happen to have an arts teacher, but every day, at every grade in every school, as a major discipline. No ifs, ands, or buts.

Disarming Aversion to the Arts

Often you'll encounter a person who is afraid that the "arts thing" is another one of the "liberal educational agendas" full of "touchy-feely" programs that vaporize when you try defend them. These critics of an arts curriculum have a concern—well, let me be more accurate—a deep fear. They fear that the arts are not as rigorous as, let's say, math. They fear students won't get the discipline of memorizing times tables. They fear the arts will compete for resources, or even that the arts might make education too enjoyable.

I have news for critics of the arts as a major discipline. Times have changed. The cries for cultural literacy and "back to basics" ignore significant evolutions in today's world. The promoters of more content per school year are living in the past. Yes, there was a time when scholars could master a good deal of what was known. It was called the Dark Ages. But information has begun doubling, again and again, faster and faster. Today, a heavily content-based curriculum makes less and less sense.

First, teachers' lectures and textbooks are no longer the primary sources of content in our world. Students are more likely to hear and see things on television or access information on the Internet. That changes the whole concept of an educational system as the source of content. Teachers can no longer stand in front of the class and tell students all the content they need to master. Filling the brain with knowledge is history. Content increases far too rapidly for mastery. Today, the "brass ring" in learning is not *what* you know, but knowing *how* to find information and how to use that information quickly, creatively, and cooperatively.

Second, high school graduation rates for the first 20 years of the 20th century were close to 25 percent. Kids typically left school after the 8th grade and went to work. But during the Great Depression, those rare and precious jobs went only to family breadwinners, and teenagers stayed in school.

By 1950 and through 1970, high school graduation rates in the United States averaged an estimated 50–70 percent. From the '70s to the end of the century, the number of graduates as a percentage of 18-year-olds remained close to 70 percent. The number of 25- to 29-year-olds with high school diplomas in 1995 rose to about 87 percent because of alternative programs such as night school (NCES, 1998).

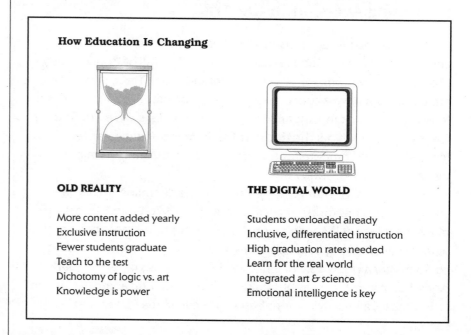

How Education Is Changing

OLD REALITY

More content added yearly
Exclusive instruction
Fewer students graduate
Teach to the test
Dichotomy of logic vs. art
Knowledge is power

THE DIGITAL WORLD

Students overloaded already
Inclusive, differentiated instruction
High graduation rates needed
Learn for the real world
Integrated art & science
Emotional intelligence is key

In the course of that increase in graduation rates, the educational agendas of the past 30 years became more inclusive. The students who *used to drop out* because of financial needs, behavior and attention disorders, poor memory, pregnancy, weak social skills, household violence, or a host of other problems, *are now in schools.* The bottom line is that so-called hard- to-reach students used to drop out. Now we are committed to helping them stay in school—and to succeed. The arts are the *best vehicle available* to do that job. This book presents data to support this claim.

Third, the Information Age is different from what you thought it was. Knowledge is no longer key now that everyone has access to it. Rolf Jensen, director of the Copenhagen Institute for Futures Studies, gives us a glimpse into this new 21st century:

> We are in the twilight of a society based on data. As information and intelligence become the domain of computers, society will place a new value on the one human ability that can't be automated: emotion (Jensen, 1999, p. 84).

He's right. For the last quarter of the 20th century, information was prized. If we could just make faster chips, we could process more information quicker. So we did. The laptop that this book was written on is more powerful than a roomful of computers from the '70s. But in the first part of a new millennium, it's not information we need. It's not content. It's not more facts, names, and concepts. Pouring more content down students' throats won't work. Advocates of more content are out of step with reality. Students today are flooded with data but often starved for meaningful learning. Students may not be able to name 10 elements from the Periodic Chart or five countries in South America, or tell you why winters are colder than summers or how to turn gallons into liters—but they'd *better* know *where* to find that information quickly. They'd better understand how to solve problems, what makes arguments plausible, how to build teams, and how to incorporate the concept of fairness into daily life. What employers are telling all of us in education is this: "We want thinkers, we want people skills, we want problem-solvers, we want creativity, and we want teamwork."

So let me translate all of those real-world, workplace demands for you: Emotional balance and cognitive flexibility will become gold (if not platinum!) That's right. At the start of this new century, for those with emotional balance and cognitive flexibility, the world will be their oyster. They will have the social skills, self-discipline, and thinking skills to thrive in a fast-changing world.

Finally, those critical of the arts are stuck in the old dichotomy between the arts and sciences. They often pit the arts and sciences against each other in meaningless, irrelevant oppositions such as touchy-feely versus high standards, right brain versus left brain, intu-ition versus logic, or enjoyment versus hard work. None of those hold up under scrutiny if you understand the brain. Studies demonstrate that both the arts and sciences use both sides of the brain and, in fact, some of the arts may use more of the brain than most science. Still, to incorpo-rate the elements that lead to better thinkers and better people, I believe elementary and secondary policymakers ought to cut the vol-ume of content in half. Students are asked to learn far too much trivia that they'll never remember past test time. Be honest with yourself. How much subject matter content do you remember from high school? Most would say under 5 percent. Let's learn not to value something just because it is easy to teach, is easy to test, and makes politicians look good.

It's not the quantity of textbook pages assigned that makes students smart. It's how they learn to think about their new learning. Can they analyze it, critique it, and place it in context? Students need to study big-ger, more difficult ques-tions and to take the time to ponder and reflect. The more challenging and ambiguous the problems, the better. The more disci-plines learning involves, the better. The longer it takes students to explore a topic, the better. We need less trivia and more in-depth learning about the things that matter the most in our world: order, integrity, thinking skills, a sense of wonder, truth, flexibili-ty, fairness, dignity, contribution, justice, creativity, and cooperation. Does that sound like a tall order? The arts can do all that. We need more of the arts because they can do *more* of that than any other discipline.

Make the goal high test scores and you get a majority of students who get higher test scores and a minority who are turned off by learning and school. Make your priority bet-ter human beings and you'll not only get bet-ter test scores, you'll also get cooperative, self-disciplined, creative, and compassionate stu-dents with a real love of learning.

The critic who wants students to focus on higher test scores is really saying, "I want someone who *values* doing well on tests. I want some-one who *feels strongly* about the long-term gains that might come from the test. I want someone who, even though he or she might have a headache or the flu, will *set their cares aside* and do well on the test."

But what does that critic really want? Isn't that critic asking educa-tors to inculcate strong shared values and the ability to self-regulate behavior? The arts can help do this. But remember that high test scores are just part of the overall set of indicators as to whether a student is doing well.

A Postscript and Foreshadowing

If you're wondering, right up front, if the arts-laden curriculum I propose will work, rest assured. One good model has been succeeding for more than 50 years: the Waldorf schools, independent, arts-centered institutions that are one of the fastest-growing educational models in the world, with 130 schools in the United States and 700 worldwide (visit the Association of Waldorf Schools of North America on the Web at http://www.awsna.org/awsna/ and search for Waldorf Schools; many schools have Web sites).

Other exemplary schools—not in the Waldorf system—include Anza Elementary School in Los Angeles; Eliot Elementary in Needham, Massachusetts; and Davidson Middle/High School in Augusta, Georgia.

At a Waldorf school, there are countless things to drive straight-line, high standards, bean-counting, highly competitive parents crazy. Waldorf teachers avoid textbooks. They heap on field trips, encourage journal reflections, downplay tests. These schools use the looping practice, where teachers stay with students for years, usually 1st through 8th grades. This places a premium on long-term relationships. Waldorf schools never force reading on students, focusing instead on love of languages and literature. Often children don't learn to read until age 7, 8, or even 9. Students often spend a whole year building a piece of furniture or a musical instrument. Valuable class time is used for community service. This kind of loosey-goosey schooling really tests the patience of anxious parents. Understandably, some panic and pull their children out of school.

But something must be working. Prominent educational figures such as Howard Gardner and Theodore Sizer admire Waldorf schools. Oppenheimer (1999) recounts a number of facts about Waldorf: On Scholastic Assessment Tests, Waldorf students *outperform* national averages. Waldorf school records are full of athletic victories over schools two or three times their size. At a local martial arts studio, the instructor muses, "In thirteen years, I've had two black belts, both Waldorf kids." Graduates commonly get into the best universities. They often pass achievement tests at double or triple the rate for public school students.

College professors remark about the humility, sense of wonder, concentration and intellectual resourcefulness of Waldorf graduates.

So what is the secret? How do small, underfunded private schools produce successful graduates like Oscar-winning actor Paul Newman, Nobel laureate and novelist Saul Bellow, and legendary dancer Mikhail Baryshnikov?

You may have guessed the answer. The Waldorf curriculum is heavily grounded in the arts. Younger students do drawings with crayons and colored pens every day. They work with puppets and dolls early on. Student notebooks are filled with notes, records, and observations from classroom experiments and field trips. Students give oral presentations nearly every day. Students hear fables and stories every day. They build wooden art objects from scratch, often taking months to complete projects.

Music is just as strong. All 1st graders learn to play a recorder, storing them in cases they build themselves. The schools offers jazz, choir, orchestra, and more. A day starts with singing and may end with a drama. Students learn math by hopping around an exercise room in a syncopated pattern. Movement, dance, and physical education are embedded throughout the curriculum.

Obviously, over the years, students learn a tremendous amount of science, literature and math. But they do it through the processes of the arts.

What does all this do for the students? Graduate Peter Nitze, who attended Waldorf then later graduated from both Harvard and Stanford, said, "If you've had the experience of binding a book, knitting a sock, playing a recorder, then you feel you can build a rocket ship—or learn a software program you've never touched. It's not a bravado, just a quiet confidence. There's nothing you can't do. . . ." By the way, Nitze is the global operations director for Allied-Signal, a multinational, billion-dollar aerospace and automotive manufacturing corporation.

■ ■ ■

Is there a lesson here for other schools? There could be—if you're looking for a way to not just raise test scores, but to raise better people, go through the doorway marked, "The Arts Taught Here."

2 Musical *Arts*

*T*his chapter broadens the discourse on the musical arts and emphasizes their value in education and our society. I offer theories on *why* music is valuable, and back up those theories with evidence. I also offer practical suggestions on what music is best and for what purposes. Before we get to the evidence, a brief reminder: I am well aware that music can lift our spirits, enlarge our souls, express the hard-to-express, and often make life worth living. But those arguments are not the focus here.

First, let's define our terms. "Musical arts" or "music-making" means much more than playing music or listening to it. Singing, rapping, and producing musicals are also part of the musical arts. In addition, the musical arts include composing music, reading music, analyzing, arranging, notating, and creating music.

Like mathematics, music has a universal language, with a symbolic way of representing the world. Again, like mathematics, the musical arts let us communicate with others—illuminate and record human insights. Musical arts are not only part of our built-in, biological design, but they may develop essential neurobiological systems. If they do, they are *far more important* than the fact that they might boost jigsaw puzzle (spatial) skills. Neurobiologist Mark Jude Tramo of Harvard Medical School says, "Music is biologically part of human life, just as music is aesthetically part of human life" (personal communication, March 13, 1999). Compelling evidence supports the hypothesis that musical arts may provide a positive, significant, and lasting benefit to learners. There is no single piece of evidence, but the diversity and depth of supporting material is overwhelming. If this were a court case, the ruling would be that music is valuable beyond reasonable doubt.

So why do we still have to fight to include music in the curriculum? The unfortunate answer is that most policymakers and politicians are interested in the input-output ratio. That's the cost per student per year against the resulting test scores—the old factory model of education. The problem is that the arts are just not efficient. Many arts-related benefits take months or years to show up. But when they do, and they always will, they roar onto center stage with brilliance. By then, it's too late for the decision makers to notice. They missed the music, again.

Making a Case for Music

It's a strong claim: *Music-making is part of what makes us human.* Frank Wilson (1999), assistant clinical professor of neurology at the University of California School of Medicine, says that learning to play an instrument connects, develops, and refines *the entire neurological and motor brain systems.* To substantiate the case that music is a fundamental, essential human discipline, this chapter makes the following arguments:

   • Music enhances our biological survival.
   • It has predictable developmental periods.
   • Cognitive systems are enhanced, including visual-spatial, analytical, mathematical, creative.
   • Emotional systems are positively affected, including endocrine, hormonal, social, personal skills, cultural and aesthetic appreciation.
   • Perceptual-motor systems are enhanced, including listening, vestibular systems, sensory acuity, timing, state management.
   • Stress response system is enhanced, which includes the immune response and autonomic nervous system, the sympathetic and parasympathetic systems.
   • Memory systems are activated through improved listening, attention, concentration and recall (see Figure 2.1).

Hard-Wired for Music

If Darwin was right, traits and behaviors that enhance the survival of a species will be selected by nature because they'll better ensure the

FIGURE 2.1
MUSIC AFFECTS MULTIPLE SYSTEMS

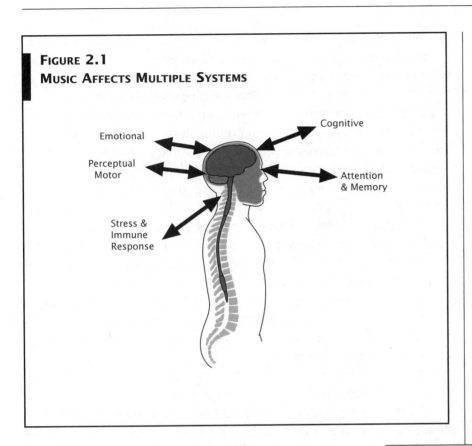

perpetuation of a species from one generation to the next. Could the use of music increase survival chances? Bjorn Merker has studied this question, and the most likely answer seems to be yes (Wallin, Merker, & Brown, 1999).

We have some clues that hint how music-making *might* have been useful for survival. Cave paintings depicting the use of music go back 70,000 years. Flutes have been found in France dating as far back as 30,000 years. Music, vocalized or played by an individual or sung as social chorus (birds, whales, or ape choruses), may have been used to attract a mate. It's possible others were attracted to those producing louder, better, or more pleasing sounds.

In addition, animals and early humans often used music for intra-group communication, which increased group safety and identification. Likely, robust vocalization improved notification of pending threat or environmental changes. Music may be used to increase harmony and social bonding among those playing it or listening to it. Music may have also contributed to changes in the brain (i.e., verbal memory,

Hypothesis:

Music is part of our biological heritage and is hard-wired into our genes as a survival strategy.

counting, and self-discipline), which may have enhanced survival. And, finally, making music probably strengthened listening skills, certainly a valued trait when hunting game or escaping predators.

The human brain appears to have highly specialized structures for music. For instance, melodic contour has corresponding brain cells that process it (Weinberger & McKenna, 1988). Researchers have found other cells in the mammalian auditory cortex that process specific harmonic relationships (Sutter & Schreiner, 1991). The rhythmic, temporal qualities have been linked to a specific group of neurons in the auditory cortex.

The ability to discern dissonant music shows up before any possible musical training could have occurred. Contrary to our intuition, even 6- to 9-month-old infants, with no musical experience, can demonstrate a kind of built-in musical awareness (Trehub, Bull, & Thorpe, 1984). Whereas other studies need to verify that it is musical versus generic dissonance, this research can make a strong case for the hypothesis that music properties may be innate. But what of people who are weak in musical skills or cannot even hear?

The 5–10 percent of the population that cannot give even a baseline performance on rudimentary musical tasks is not well studied at this time. It is likely that the qualities of music are always represented in the brain, but some mechanism may simply inhibit the body's response to those musical qualities (e.g., marching, singing, smiling). Most evidence hints that musical talent is more than just listening; it engages the whole body. Though no one observation in this section is proof, taken in concert, there is a strong case for the biological basis of music.

Music Has Developmental Periods

Hypothesis:

The research on music points to a genetically and environmentally influenced mechanism in place at birth.

If an ability or talent is built in, then it is either mature at birth or it develops over time. Several recent articles and books have suggested that learning music has a critical period early in life. The brain does have some periods that are more sensitive than others to the active development of music. It optimally makes sense to engage learners during that time. But research *does not* say that if you don't learn music as a youngster, you'll never learn it. Research does suggest that *when you learn* will affect how much time it takes you to learn it and how proficient you may get.

Music Prior to Birth

There's clear evidence of an *in utero* response to music. At this early stage of research on the effects of music *in utero,* it may be better to take a cautious stance. There's no evidence that *in utero* exposure to Mozart or any other composer has benefits. Protect the unborn child from any loud music. Stick with normal or soft voices, soft instrumentals, and lullabies.

Birth to 2 Years

At this time, the neurons in the auditory cortex are *highly plastic and adaptive.* Even 5-month-old infants can discriminate between the smallest interval used in Western music, a semitone. Infants ages 8–11 months perceive and remember melodic contour. A research team confirmed an infant preference for original music as written versus altered versions (Krumhans & Juscyzk, 1990). Although this skill is not very sophisticated, researchers believe the skill begins very early. The plasticity is so strong that one study demonstrated that when implanted early enough, cochlear auditory implants can help deaf kittens hear. This finding suggests that congenitally deaf children *may be able to develop hearing* if the intervention is early enough (Klinke et al., 1999).

Ages 2–5: Early Childhood Music

Music clearly has a developmental path, with age-dependent changes. In very young children who use their left hand to play an instrument, there's evidence of larger cortical area in the sensory cortex

Practical Suggestions

In general . . . Use simple songs and lullabies. After birth, the first orientation to music is typically the mother's lullaby. Infants are very accurate in identifying their mother's voice and songs as compared to others. Infants like upbeat, major-key instrumentals at low to moderate volume at this age. By age 12–24 months, infants are ready for head nodding, clapping, and tapping. Watch an infant respond to rhythm and you'll realize the early stages of readiness. Use rhythm in your voice.

Close to age 1, simple instruments are important. These include toy whistles, harmonicas, drums, xylophones, and bells. A good CD for this age is *Baby Needs Beethoven.* You might also experiment with Disney movie soundtracks, such as *Snow White and the Seven Dwarfs, Bambi, Dumbo, Mary Poppins, Winnie the Pooh,* and Gilbert and Sullivan music. A good sourcebook is *All Ears: How to Choose and Use Recorded Music for Children,* by Jill Jarnow (1991).

Practical Suggestions

In general . . . Children are ready for sticks, shakers, and drums. Also, this is the age for making the music as social and fun as possible. Kids love silly, wacky songs because their brain's language skills have developed enough to decipher most of the words; and they appreciate alliteration and rhyme. Red Grammar's *Peace* CD is a good example.

Play clapping games, where students match your clap and create their own versions of keeping pace to music. For some children the more simple drums, sticks, kazoos, and shakers are all that's needed to start the rhythm and musical interest. Others will be ready to learn to play a keyboard, recorder, or violin. The secret is to encourage and model while still being persistent and light-hearted. Teach children to memorize Mother Goose rhymes (they have rhythm!). Kids like funny songs, too.

corresponding to the index. It's likely that the same effect would happen to the other hand, too. But those who began to play *prior to age 5* showed the greatest changes, suggesting a model for critical periods of somasensory development through music instruction (Schlaug, Jancke, & Pratt, 1995b).

At what ages should children be introduced to various kinds of music lessons? It depends partly on the maturity of the child. In general, children at age 3 are ready for simple keyboard practice. Suzuki violin practice begins at age 3 for some children, 4 for others. Children will often be out of tune, but that's fine at this age. Some children are ready for kazoos; others are ready for the wind instrument called a *recorder*. Young children's brains are forging novel neural networks and needs a high amount of exposure to a wide variety of sounds. To keep it fun, parents should model playing music, and it should be a social experience.

Begin exposing children to wider varieties of music by ages 2 and 3. They especially like folk songs, musicals, easy-to-hear pop songs, nursery rhymes, Samba, marches, Irish jig, flamenco, and traditional music. This is the time to introduce children to singing. By age 4, it's smart to include a lot of rhythm games. The brain's left hemisphere is developed more by this age, so rhythm skills improve. Encourage, as much as you can, the use of swinging, bouncing, swaying, tapping, circling, and marching to music. Maybe the best music for young children is a Sousa march that engages the whole body, the mind, and the emotions.

Music at Ages 5–10

Ideally, children would start music lessons between the age of 3 and 8, depending on maturity. Today's evidence shows that all ages are good for starting music lessons, but the *sooner the better*. If one starts early, one may benefit from enhanced interhemispheric brain activity for auditory processing. Magnetic resonance imaging (MRI) studies have shown that the fibers in the corpus callosum, which connect the left- and right-brain hemispheres, are as much as 15 percent larger in musicians compared to nonmusicians (Schlaug, Jancke, Huang, Staiger, & Steinmetz, 1995a). But this *only occurred* when the adults started playing before the age of 8. To optimize skill development, it appears to be necessary to start early. All world-class pianists began playing before they were 10 years of age.

Some evidence indicates we may be missing out on an enormous amount of talent by not encouraging student composing. When given a chance, school-age children can and will produce quality work. A rigorous study (described in Kratus, 1989) with nonmusical children ages 7, 9, and 11 years old provided some genuine insights into the processes of music composition. Each student was given a keyboard and 10 minutes to compose an original work. Keeping things easy, they all started with middle C and used only the white keys. Researchers tallied the time spent on exploration, development, and practice. All were able to create successfully novel compositions. Whereas the 7-year-olds spent the most time on exploration, the 9–11-year-olds spent more time on development and practice. That may be because the brains of the older children have developed more frontal lobe maturation and increased bridging of the corpus callosum. This maturation allows for greater complexity and the ability to juggle abstractions.

But that wasn't the most interesting part. Kratus (1994) did a follow-up study years later. This time he was investigating the creative process of children's compositions. What he discovered is that the audiation (the ability to create and hear a piece in your head) is present in 9-year-olds. This process is critical because it is the ability to try out a musical possibility without actually having to compose it. In essence, your brain becomes a musical "sketchpad." This process is identical to that used by professional musicians and suggests that we may have been underrating the creative ability of our students. Students like to compose and will do it if given the chance. By age 9 they have the basic mental processes in place that musicians have: perception, rhythm, and tonal skills.

Music at Ages 10 and Over

How much music can anyone learn starting at age 10? By this age, the musical brain is 80 percent matured. The immature areas of the brain include the frontal lobes and some remaining maturation of the corpus callosum. Under some conditions one may still begin after 10 and become a highly competent musician. Chances are remote you'll become world class; but that's rarely the objective. By age 20, the adult brain is mature. Most adults can become, with sufficient training and practice, competent on most instruments. It should be remembered

Start Early Music Training Between Ages 3 and 6

Practical Suggestions

In general . . . Read poetry that is highly rhythmical like that of Jack Prelutsky and Tom Glazer. Keyboard, piano, violin, or recorder are all great instruments at this age for training. Children are also ready, as they approach 8 and 9, to try their hand at composing simple music. Get *Good Music, Brighter Children* by Sharlene Habermeyer (1999). This is the time to introduce reggae, classical, romantic, hip-hop, and pop. Soundtracks to Disney movies, especially the pre-1960 ones, provide exposure to classical, romantic, and other musical genres.

that the nonmusical benefits (satisfaction, memory, creativity, appreciation, and self-discipline) may be as great as or greater than the more obvious skills acquired (see *Champions of Change,* Fiske, 1999, p. 10).

Singing is always appropriate for those who show interest: with bands, musicals, school choirs or barbershop-style quartets. At the middle and high school level, encourage kids to be a role model in music practice for their younger siblings. The key here is support. Make sure you support the training your children began earlier, as well as the listening skills that enhance other perceptual motor activities. Take your young teens to good-quality concerts—not just the popular teen genres. Watch the movie *Shine* with kids and discuss it afterwards.

Music Enhances Cognition Systems

Hypothesis:

Music-making contributes to the development of essential cognitive systems, which include reasoning, creativity, thinking, decision making, and problem solving.

Music helps you think by activating and synchronizing neural firing patterns that orchestrate and connect multiple brain sites. The neural synchrony ensembles increase both the brain's efficiency and effectiveness. These key systems are well connected and located in the frontal, parietal, and temporal lobes, as well as the cerebellum. The strongest studies support the value of music-making in spatial reasoning, creativity, and generalized mathematical skills.

Music and IQ Correlations

How does music enhance cognition? University of California-Irvine physicist Gordon Shaw (2000) hypothesizes that the activation between family groups of cortical neurons assist the cortex in pattern recognition. This multiple-site, cross-activation may be necessary for higher brain functions, including music, cognition, and memory. Though far from universally accepted, a basic theory of neuronal ensembles is gaining support from others in relation to other sensory and motor areas (e.g., Calvin, 1996). Patterns of a neural symphony form a plausible model that suggests music has a fast track to engaging and enhancing higher brain activities.

A Russian study (Malyarenko et al., 1996) affirms that listening to music just an hour a day may change brain reorganization. The experimental music group of 4-year-olds heard one hour a day of classical music. When later measured, their electroencephalogram (EEG) readouts showed greater brain coherence and more time spent in the alpha state. This body of data hints that music does influence not just brain activity, but coherence. This may be the "neural symphony" that Shaw was proposing.

Hellmuth Petsche (1993) of the University of Vienna found a surprising coherence of patterns at multiple sites during the tasks, revealing the global influence of music on the brain. If this theory that music might be inducing more activity among all areas of the brain (known as "coherence") is correct, then females should have greater EEG coherence, because they have more interhemispheric connections, particularly in the smaller connecting tissue between hemispheres, the anterior commissure (Allen & Gorski, 1991). In one study, scientists found that not only did musicians have far greater coherence compared to nonmusicians, but also females had higher coherence than males (Johnson et al., 1996). One study showed that neural patterns and their sequences may be the building blocks for understanding, appreciating, and engaging music (Sarntheim et al., 1998).

Music and Math Skills

Because of the traditional associations of math with music, there ought to be an overlap with music and math connections to the areas of the brain that process each of them. The key "math areas" of the brain are in the left temporal lobes, an area highly involved with music (Dehaene et al., 1999). This discovery begs the question, "Does music enhance math, or is it the math that enhances music?" Shaw's group (Graziano, Peterson, & Shaw, 1999) did an interesting experiment to find out the impact of music on math. If music affects our ability to understand proportions, math scores should improve. Shaw's four-month experiment compared three groups of 2nd graders:

- 29 received piano instruction + math video game.
- 29 received computer-based English training + math video game.
- 28 received no piano, no video (control group).

Two groups had a math video game designed to enhance spatial skills. The results were impressive. The math video game, designed by Shaw to increase spatial-proportional skills, boosted math scores by 36 percent over the control group. But the group that *also took piano lessons,* scored an additional 15 percent higher than the other experimental group, which got no music instruction. Showing a differential in

Music Activates Multiple Brain Sites

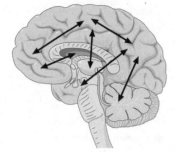

the kind of neural pathways developed, the piano group scored a striking 27 percent higher on the 16 questions that were spatially oriented (Graziano et al., 1999). This study suggests that the piano playing strengthened the spatial awareness plus the ability to think ahead—both important math skills. This makes sense; there is some overlap in the brain areas that are activated for playing music and solving math problems (see Figure 2.2).

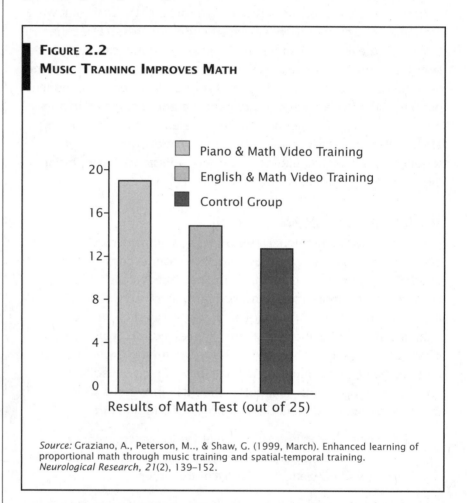

FIGURE 2.2
MUSIC TRAINING IMPROVES MATH

Legend:
- Piano & Math Video Training
- English & Math Video Training
- Control Group

Results of Math Test (out of 25)

Source: Graziano, A., Peterson, M.., & Shaw, G. (1999, March). Enhanced learning of proportional math through music training and spatial-temporal training. *Neurological Research, 21*(2), 139–152.

What would happen if you increased time on music instruction at the expense of time on math? Professor Spychiger of the University of Fribourg in Switzerland studied 70 classes for children (7–15 years old) and arranged five daily 45-minute music lessons for half the classes (see Farrell, 1973). The other half, the control group, continued to get their usual *one music lesson per week.* Surprisingly, the 35 experimental classes who took a curriculum that *increased* music instruction at the expense of language and math actually got better at language and reading. In fact, they did as well as those who spent more time on mathematics, but had no music instruction!

UCLA professor of education James Catterall is interested in the relationship between music and overall academic achievement. In particular, he was interested in what happens with the students of lower socioeconomic status who took music lessons in grades 8–12, compared to similar students who took no music lessons. First, the students who took music increased their math scores significantly as compared to the nonmusic control group. But just as important, reading, history, geography and even social skills soared by 40 percent. Music-making not only supports the development of math skills, but of all skills, for all kinds of students (Catterall et al., 1999; see Figure 2.3).

Practical Suggestions

In general . . . Encourage both music training and playful training (like video games) in the spatial skills. How much and how long should we devote to music in the schools? Early indications are that positive results take *three or more* days a week, *at least* 30 minutes a day. Optimally, students will get closer to 60 minutes a day, three to five days a week.

FIGURE 2.3
AREAS OF MATH AND MUSIC OVERLAP

PM = playing music/familiar/using piano
PS = problem-solving/spatial-abstract

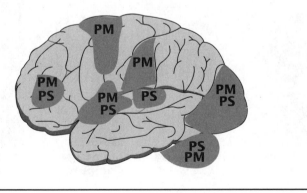

A Breakthrough Study

Increased scores in spatial-temporal reasoning ability, which is considered a key building block for higher math skills (specifically, geometric and topological skills), were results of a well-publicized experiment with 78 preschool children in Southern California. The ethnically diverse 42 boys and 36 girls were in the normal range of intelligence and had no prior musical background. The study was conducted over a two-year period in three schools; it involved either one or two lessons per week, one hour a day. There were four conditions: piano keyboard lessons, computer training, singing, and the control (see Figure 2.4).

In the area of spatial-temporal reasoning (object assembly), the results were dramatic. The keyboarding group produced a significantly

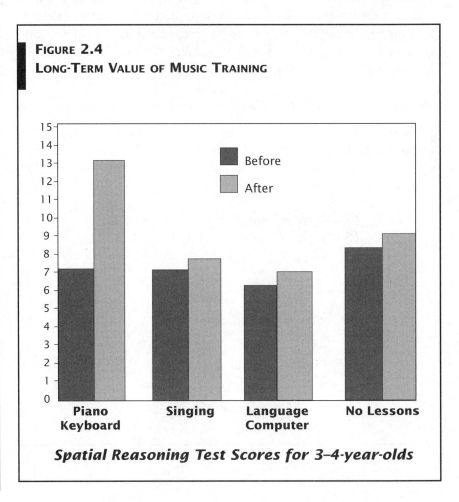

FIGURE 2.4
LONG-TERM VALUE OF MUSIC TRAINING

Spatial Reasoning Test Scores for 3–4-year-olds

higher score, 30 percent over controls, well outpacing the no-lessons, computer, and singing groups (Rauscher et al., 1997). The skill was present three days after the experiment was over, but continued music practice may be important to maintain the benefits.

Understanding the Mozart Effect

The entire hoopla surrounding the so-called Mozart IQ effect is another case of someone looking for a cheap, "get-smart quick" scheme. In the infamous University of California-Irvine study, college students used headsets to listen to either white noise, relaxation music, or Mozart for 10 minutes. Afterwards, the Mozart group performed better on spatial tasks than those in the other two groups. The authors of the original study never claimed any more than a temporary (10-minute) effect, and it was only in certain spatial skills (Rauscher, Shaw, & Ky, 1993).

Lawrence Parsons of the University of Texas at San Antonio's Health Science Research Imaging Center wondered: (1) Was it Mozart or the components of Mozart that made the effect? and (2) Could other kinds of "primers" (like pump primers; e.g., visual vs. auditory stimuli) work better than Mozart? His results were intriguing. Each of the micro musical components—pitch, melody, and beat (rhythm)—bettered Mozart in the spatially oriented cube comparison (object rotation). They were better by up to 30 percent, with complex rhythm almost *three times as helpful as Mozart*. Even a rhythmic rain forest background beat Mozart. This discovery suggests that the basic individual elements of music may be better than the integrated whole for other simple tasks (Parsons, Martinez, Delosh, Halpern, & Thaut, in press; see Figure 2.5).

The study by Parsons and colleagues (2000) also suggests we should consider the value of matching the *modality* of the stimulus with the *modality* of the task. For example, a visual primer (like watching a screen saver full of collapsing boxes or being forced to make visual estimates of size, volume, or length) is far superior than sound alone (even listening to Mozart) if the task primarily requires visual skills (like cube comparisons). Second, it may not necessarily be Mozart (although it works to a degree) that temporarily enhances certain spatial skills; it's the more fundamental building block of rhythm that may be doing it. What's more, other music elements may enhance other learning tasks. For example, what type of music would best enhance writing skills? That would be a good action research project.

Practical Suggestions

In general . . . Short-term listening can produce a temporary (5–15 minutes) gain in select spatial skills. For lasting gains, nothing (so far) beats music training that starts early and continues for at least a year. *Elementary level:* Playing a keyboard (or piano) is the only instrument tested that we know increases spatial-temporal reasoning development. In the classroom, teachers can use clapping or rhythm games, as well as playing CDs of rhythmic music (e.g., disco music) and letting students learn to the beat of the music.

Practical Suggestions

In general . . . Set up action research with your own students. You'll know what works with your students only if you experiment with this music. *Elementary and secondary levels:* Work with another teacher; divide your class in half. Switch the two halves, so you have half of your students and half of another teacher's students. You both do a 10-minute "primer," but with differ-ent selections of music. For example, you might use a more rhythmic selection of drumbeats, and the other teacher might use Mozart's Sonata for Two Pianos in D Major. Then switch back, and both groups, now mixed, do the task. Measure the results. You may be the one who discovers the next music genre for a priming effect. As a general rule, between 10 and 30 percent of the time, music makes good sense.

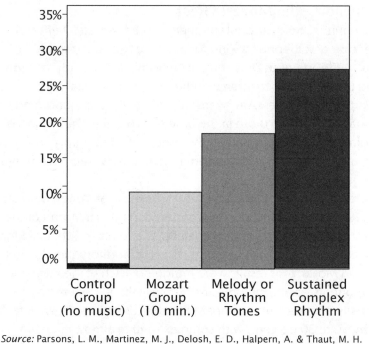

FIGURE 2.5
TEMPORARY INCREASE IN SPATIAL REASONING (OBJECT ROTATION) SCORES OVER BASELINE

Source: Parsons, L. M., Martinez, M. J., Delosh, E. D., Halpern, A. & Thaut, M. H. (2000). *Musical and visual priming of visualization and mental rotation.* Manuscript submitted for publication.

Part of the direct value of playing music comes from gains in spatial reasoning, a building block for proportional math. Unless students master proportions and the ability to create, hold, and manipulate objects and space, they'll be stuck having to master every bit of math by memorization. They'll never get to the higher levels of math because one could never memorize the infinite combinations and relationships. This critical spatial-cognitive sense allows learners to progress into fields such as engineering, robotics, design, statistics, construction, art, genetics, and all fields that involve comparisons and symmetrical relationships.

Music in the Background

Does music in the background enhance learning performance? In a 1952 study, 278 eighth and ninth graders were tested with background music in a study hall. They had better reading comprehension than the

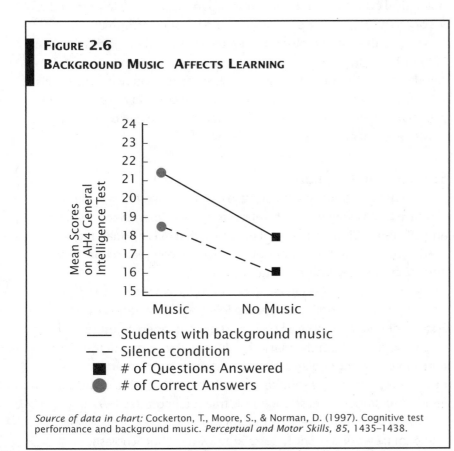

FIGURE 2.6
BACKGROUND MUSIC AFFECTS LEARNING

—— Students with background music
– – Silence condition
■ # of Questions Answered
● # of Correct Answers

Source of data in chart: Cockerton, T., Moore, S., & Norman, D. (1997). Cognitive test performance and background music. *Perceptual and Motor Skills, 85,* 1435–1438.

Practical Suggestions

In general . . . The best background music must be predictable, so that it does not distract. *Elementary and secondary levels:* You might consider popular jazz instrumentalists like George Benson, Kenny G, or David Sanborn. Environmental music can work wonders, too. Consider using ocean sound, waterfall, or rain forest soundtracks. In addition, baroque music can work well if it meets the following criteria: (1) it is composed in a major key; (2) it is done with orchestras, not individual instruments; and (3) the movements are *adagio* or *andante*. This music is characterized by balance and predictability. Composers (Baroque era) who have predictability and balance to their music are Bach (*Brandenburg Concertos*), Handel (*Water Music*), and Vivaldi (*Four Seasons*).

control group (Hall, 1952). In a 1997 study, 30 undergraduates were tested with a repeated-and-reversed study design. This meant that the two conditions (music and no music) were repeated for the same group, then reversed so that each group got the other condition. Those listening to the music outperformed those in the silence condition (Figure 2.6). The researcher believed that the music may facilitate a more focused thinking for general intelligence, not just spatial skills (Cockerton, Moore, & Norman, 1997).

Practical Suggestions

In general . . . Music that stimulates creativity is different from the predictable and balanced genres for background. Use these expressive and innovative musical types to stimulate ideas before or during challenging tasks. *Elementary level:* Use John Cage (*Three Constructions*), Duke Ellington (*The Ellington Suites*) and Berlioz (*Symphonie Fantastique*). Secondary level: Use Peter Gabriel (*Passion*), Isaac Hayes (*Hot Buttered Soul*), Bud Powell (*The Best of Bud Powell on Verve*), The Kronos Quartet (*Pieces of Africa*), and Beethoven (*Fifth Symphony*).

Creativity and Music

Many researchers have reported that creativity is enhanced by music. For instance, one study found that a year of music instruction significantly increased creativity (Wolff, 1979). The control class received no musical education, and the music group received 30 minutes a day for one year. Students were tested on the Purdue Perceptual-Motor Survey and the Torrance Tests of Creativity. This study suggests the value of long-term music programs versus a one-time hit-or-miss approach. Another study found that classical music enhances visual imagery skills (McKinney & Tims, 1995). In a third study, the creativity to embellish potential solutions to mock social problem was enhanced by the use of music (Bryan et al., 1998).

Summary on Cognition

The neural symphony theory says that music may activate and synchronize brain activity. This correlates to greater learner engagement and efficiency. There's no causal evidence that music equals higher grades because of the tremendous number of complex school variables. But some facts deserve stating.

Asian countries like Taiwan, Singapore, Japan rank among the top countries in the world in math and science scores, whereas the United States ranks near the bottom on the list of developed countries. Are Asian students inherently smarter? Culture is always part of the equation, but music might play a big role. In Japan (as in other countries near the top), music is a required, equal, major discipline in the curriculum and all students get strong music training in grades 1–9.

The College Board reports that for the 1999–2000 school year, music coursework is strongly correlated with higher Scholastic Assessment Test (SAT) scores. Students with just a half-year of arts coursework averaged a 7- and 10-point gain in verbal and math respectively. But after four years of coursework in music, students averaged 49 points higher on the combined (and averaged) verbal and math SAT scores (Music Educators National Conference, MENC, 2000;[1] see Figure 2.7). This suggests that music over the long haul provides the greatest bene-

---

[1]*Note:* To find information and tables about SAT scores on the Web, go to the College Board's (2000) Web site (http://www.collegeboard.org/prof/), click the "Search" button at the top, and enter "national report" in the box. Then scroll through the items to find the *National Report for College-Bound Seniors* for the years 1998, 1999, and 2000. MENC (2000) gives these reports as a source for the data in Figure 2.7.

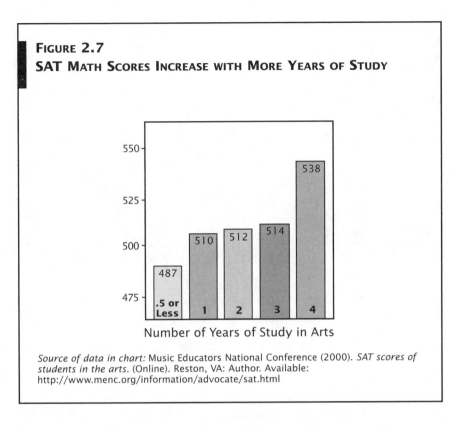

FIGURE 2.7
SAT MATH SCORES INCREASE WITH MORE YEARS OF STUDY

Number of Years of Study in Arts

Source of data in chart: Music Educators National Conference (2000). *SAT scores of students in the arts.* (Online). Reston, VA: Author. Available: http://www.menc.org/information/advocate/sat.html

fit, because scores *increase* each year students are involved with arts. These are correlations, not causal evidence. But, remember, there is no causal evidence that courses in other disciplines (e.g., English or math) raise SAT scores. Music-making stands well above other disciplines in its likely effect on overall learning.

Music Enhances Emotional Intelligence

If this hypothesis is correct, we should be able to find physical links from the musical activation areas to these emotional systems. The recent awareness of emotional intelligence has reminded all of us that the benefits of cognition and expressions of emotion are intertwined. An area in the midbrain, the nucleus basalis, gives a weighted emotional meaning to our auditory input and codes it as important and worth storing in long-term memory. It is not surprising that music plays an important role in emotional intelligence.

> *Hypothesis:*
>
> Music activates and develop the areas most involved in our brains that facilitate mood, social skills, motivational development, cultural awareness, self-discipline and personal management, and aesthetic appreciation.

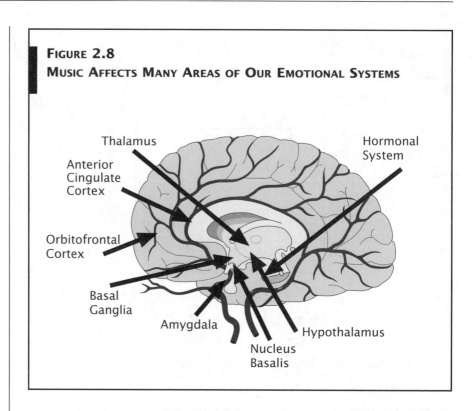

FIGURE 2.8
MUSIC AFFECTS MANY AREAS OF OUR EMOTIONAL SYSTEMS

The most likely mechanisms for developing emotional intelligence are neural networks. These are the complex patterns of neurons that comprise our behaviors. Neural nets begin as a simple sensory activation. But neurons later connect other neurons, often as many as 10,000–50,000 at a time. They decide which other neurons to connect with and stick with through both genetic and environmental stimuli. Because music evokes emotions, the playing of music accelerates and enhances the ability of learners to make these rapid emotional assessments and to act accordingly.

Earlier studies have consistently demonstrated that music-making engages multiple brain sites (see Figure 2.8). We also know music-making may contribute to developing smarter neural networks. Our emotional system regulates a great deal of our effectiveness and satisfaction in life and may be just as important in life to our success as cognition (Goleman, 1995). As with the other hypotheses, it should be noted that this high-speed path to emotional effectiveness through music-making is not causal, but highly correlated.

Identifying Emotions

The American Music Therapy Association has been a significant force in the research, implementation, and public dissemination of knowledge in this growing field. Predictably, there are studies which show that music can be used as a therapeutic tool. With musical experience, we ought to be better able to detect and respond to emotions. One study suggests that music improves emotional awareness (Alexander & Beatty, 1996). Notably, early music exposure may help children identify and manage their own emotional states. In another study, children with music exposure were able more to accurately identify their emotions. John Kratus (1989) at Case Western Reserve tested a group of 5–12-year-olds (with no musical training) and showed they could differentiate among happy, sad, and excited passages from Bach's 30 *Goldberg Variations.*

Social and Emotional Skills

The University of Fribourg study mentioned earlier showed that music instruction enhanced both social skills and academic skills (Farrell, 1973). In a separate study, music used in games enhanced general competence and self-concept (Morton et al., 1998). For youngsters who are developmentally delayed or suffer from other problems like autism, music seems to aid in the development of social skills. In one study, developmentally delayed (autistic children were in this group) and normal 6–9-year-olds were taught with music integrated into their social play. Music was found to contribute substantially to both groups in their ability to follow directions and engage in social play. With the delayed children, lowered stress levels were noted, possibly because of an improved ability to participate correctly (Edgerton, 1994).

When music was used in the background with a group of 27 preschool children, more child-to-child interactions occurred (Godeli et al., 1996). In another study, developmentally delayed children were successfully integrated with normal children (ages 3–5) through the use of music therapy. The music enabled youngsters to relax and perform better in social interactions (Gunsberg, 1991).

Can Music Have Negative Effects?

Many students who seem attracted to heavy metal or violent rap music may already be predisposed to inappropriate behaviors. In a

Practical Suggestions.

In general . . . Use music with wide variations and dissonance. *Elementary level:* Try *Renaissance of the Celtic Harp, Blue Danube* by Strauss, *Romeo and Juliet,* "None But the Lonely Heart Prelude" (Tchaikovsky), "Love-Death" (from Wagner's *Tristan und Isolde*), and Handel's *Water Music. Secondary level:* Consider using movie soundtracks. The best ones are the original scores, not the complication of pop, rap, or rock hits. Try "Lara's Theme" from *Dr. Zhivago;* "Love Theme" from *Exodus; Verismo,* Arias sung—and conducted—by José Cura; themes from *My Own Story; Bravo Pavarotti; Scheherazade.* Experiment with music from the movies *Terms of Endearment, The Mission, On Golden Pond, Shawshank Redemption, Life Is Beautiful,* and *Titanic*). Composers such as Wagner, Chopin, and Tchaikovsky are excellent.

study of young male felony offenders, rap music was most commonly cited as their favorite (Gardstrom, 1999). But that's not causal evidence. Narrative comments by the subjects suggested that music was more a reflection of their lives than a call to action. Only 4 percent thought the music was causal in their behavior, although 72 percent said that their moods were influenced by music. A separate study of 121 high school students suggested that although heavy metal fans espoused fewer compelling reasons for living and had more thoughts of suicide, subjects also claimed that the music elevated their moods (Scheel & Westefeld, 1999). As has been suggested before, listening to heavy metal music is not causal in suicides or inappropriate behavior, though it raises a red flag for potential destructive behavior (see Took & Weiss, 1994).

Summary on Emotions and Music

Music can assist us in creating, identifying, and using emotional states to regulate our lives. Musicians use music to communicate, and a good performance or song will communicate emotions. We understand ourselves better when we can express ourselves through alternative media like music. Music-making forces us to create, reflect, bare our souls, ponder, react, and formulate in ways we have never done before. It's a powerful language of expression, whether a student is playing or listening to it. In summary, music-making enhances the systems that allow us to perceive and respond appropriately to a world rich with emotions and complex social structures.

Music Enhances Perceptual-Motor Systems

Hypothesis:

Music may strengthen our ability to perceive sensory information and act on it.

Hearing selected sounds, playing an instrument, and singing may improve our ability to make finer acoustic distinctions and related auditory refinements. These qualities can positively influence a variety of skills, especially listening and reading. The effects are a result of the physical reorganization and growth in brain areas that define and regulate these skills. Such improvement has lifelong implications, including a significant and lasting effect on our perceptual abilities.

If there's a change in our behavior, there's a corresponding change in the physical nature of our brain. The presence of auditory cortical

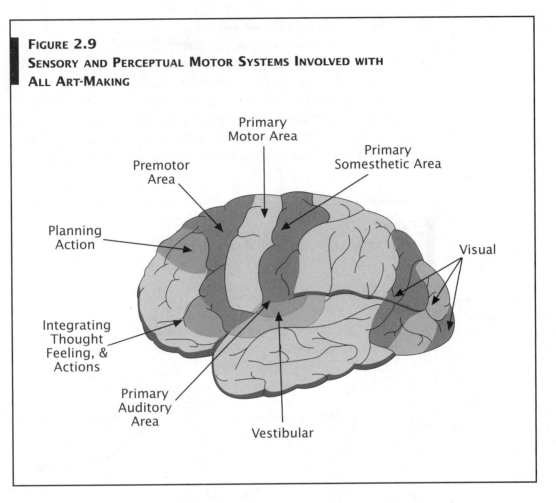

FIGURE 2.9
SENSORY AND PERCEPTUAL MOTOR SYSTEMS INVOLVED WITH ALL ART-MAKING

Premotor Area

Primary Motor Area

Primary Somesthetic Area

Planning Action

Visual

Integrating Thought Feeling, & Actions

Primary Auditory Area

Vestibular

maps has been known for quite some time. New neural connections (synapses) are made when the brain is being enriched by novelty, challenge, repetition, feedback, coherence, and having sufficient time to make the changes (see Figure 2.9).

UCLA neuroscientist Arnold Scheibel tells the story of an autopsy he did on a renowned violinist. The area of the brain responsible for hearing reception (layer four, auditory cortex) was twice as thick as normal (reported by Diamond & Hopson, 1998). A subsequent study on the part of the cortex involved with speech suggests that postnatal experience with sounds does enhance cell changes (Simonds & Scheibel, 1989). This encouraged other researchers to look for changes in the brain as a response to music-making.

How Music Changes the Brain

Playing an instrument can literally change the brain. The cerebellum, another area of the brain we know to be involved, particularly in keeping beat and rhythm, was larger in musicians (Schlaug et al., 1995b). Schlaug compared the cerebellum volume in 90 musicians and 90 nonmusicians. His team discovered that, on the average, the cerebella of musicians was 5 percent larger than those of nonmusicians. This suggests that many years of extra finger exercise prompted additional

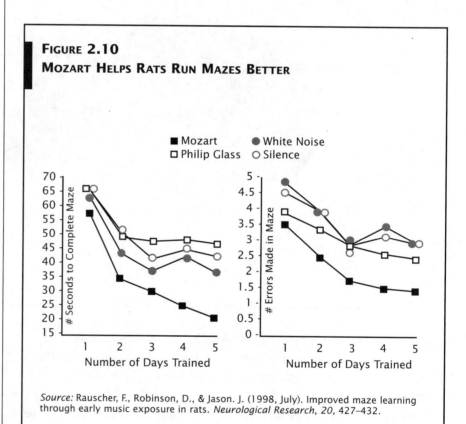

FIGURE 2.10
MOZART HELPS RATS RUN MAZES BETTER

■ Mozart   ● White Noise
□ Philip Glass   ○ Silence

Source: Rauscher, F., Robinson, D., & Jason. J. (1998, July). Improved maze learning through early music exposure in rats. *Neurological Research, 20*, 427–432.

nerve growth. In a study of string players, those who had practiced for the longest had the greatest changes in their brains (Pantev et al., 1998). There are also physical differences in the corpus callosum. It's as much as 15 percent larger in musicians than in nonmusicians (Schlaug et al., 1995a).

Music and Reading

If the physical brain is changed through music, do those changes influence other auditory perceptual skills, such as speaking, reading, and following directions? A study of 1st graders, matched for age, IQ, and socioeconomic status, suggests that music facilitates reading. The experimental group of children received music instruction for 40 minutes a day, five days a week, for seven months. They were tested on reading ability at the outset and the end, and the same teachers were used for both the control and experimental group. The music group scored higher (88th percentile vs. the 72nd percentile) in both the first and second years (Hurwitz et al., 1975). Other studies suggest that music may facilitate awareness and discrimination of sounds, key skills needed for reading. They also found a high correlation between how well children could read and their pitch discrimination.

Visual-motor skills were enhanced in another study. Children from 3–6 years old, 58 total, were placed in two groups. One group received Suzuki music instruction; the control group did not. After four months, both groups were tested for visual-motor skills, and those in the music group scored higher. This may indicate a solid transfer effect from the music instruction. But did prior music background bias that study? A study by Mozart Effect™ codiscoverer, Francis Rauscher, on rats (with no musical background), showed improved maze-running when exposed to music versus nonmusical controls (Rauscher, Robinson, & Jason, 1998; see Figure 2.10). This finding is intriguing. In mammals that do not get any exposure to music, prolonged music exposure improved their intelligence, compared to those who get no music exposure. Although it's not a human study, it suggests that music may have some long-term effects on intelligence.

Singing and Cognition

Would singing benefit students' academic performance? In Hungary, where math and science scores top the those of the United States by a wide margin, the Kodaly Method emerged from the work of Zoltan Kodaly. The Kodaly schools use a method of singing in perfect pitch, starting with folk songs. Later, students read any piece of music and sing something that was composed for an instrument in perfect pitch. This attention to sounds pays off. The Kodaly Method has grown worldwide, and the students become good overall learners (for more

Practical Suggestions

In general . . . If you are listening to music while a text is being read, the music must match the emotional intensity and pacing of the text. Pick music with distinct highs and lows. *Elementary level:* Soundtracks are good; so is music from the Romantic era like *Peter and the Wolf* by Tchaikovsky. *Secondary level:* If the music is simply in the background, you'll want highly predictable, nondistracting music, like *Four Seasons*, "*Spring*" (Vivaldi), *Water Music* (Handel) *Breezin'* (George Benson), *Brandenburg Concertos* (Bach), *Eine Kleine Nachtmusik* (Mozart), *Music for Accelerated Learning* (Halpern), *Environmental Music* (Natural Sounds), *Hot Buttered Soul* (Isaac Hayes), and Beethoven.

Practical Suggestions

In general . . . Get your students involved with school or religious choirs, or encourage them to create their own group! Elementary level: Almost any singing is helpful before age 12. But wait until that age to begin any vocal training to avoid strains or damage. Traditional songs are great for singing ("I've Been Working on the Railroad" or "She'll Be Comin' 'Round the Mountain"). Hap Palmer songs and Disney ones are also great sing-alongs. For choir listening as a warm-up to singing, it's tough to beat George Frideric Handel's "Hallelujah Chorus." Other fabulous selections include *An English Ladymass* (Anonymous), *The Emma Kirby Collection,* and *Music for St. Anthony of Padua* by Guillaume Dufay.

information, see Organization of American Kodaly Educators, OAKE, 2000).

As another example, the popular press often features the Boys Choir of Harlem, in New York City (Barnet, 2000; Gregorian, 1997). The choir is part of the Choir Academy of Harlem, a grade 4–12 arts academy (director, Walter Turnbull). About 3,000 boys try out for the academy every year, but only 150 are accepted. The group sings for presidents, at Carnegie Hall, at Academy Awards shows, and other events. Membership means extra work every day to participate. Does this activity add to student workloads and reduce time for keeping up in their studies? Yes—but it seems to motivate them to work harder. The Harlem group's results are attention getting. Over 90 percent of the participants in the Boys Choir go to college; last year, 98 percent of high school graduates went on to college (Barnet).

If music enhances perceptual-motor systems, then there also ought to be effects with those cognitively delayed. In a group of 2–5-year-olds, 10 weeks of singing reportedly increased test scores. The students tested were developmentally delayed in vocabulary and language and did have related musical activities with the singing (Hoskins, 1988). In normal children, a study was done with 3-year-olds who got twice-weekly instruction over a three-year period. The control group got regular preschool programs. There were no measurable differences in IQ scores, typically weighted toward math and memory. The other results, however, were remarkable. The singing experimental group improved motor development coordination, abstract conceptual thinking, improvisation, verbal abilities, and creativity (Kalmar, 1982).

Muscle Control, Strength, and Endurance

Music performance can affect a half-dozen nonmusical skills, including an internal time-keeper, fine-motor skills, and memory (Palmer, C., 1997). Many researchers are now using music (combined with visualization) as a way to regulate movement (e.g., Chase, 1993). The results have been positive. Music has assisted runners in improving training times. Among competitive swimmers, music has improved performance. Other studies have supported the prudent and purposeful use of music for exercise enhancement. The heavy, pumping rhythmic music enhances strength; and the calming, relaxing, soothing music actually weakens our muscle strength. These studies and others suggest that music gets at the core of our rhythms, motivation, and overall performance.

Summary on Perceptual-Motor Enhancement

For most of us, it's revolutionary to find out that listening to or making music is not just for fun or to make you smarter, but can make you better at what you do. The systems that are enhanced by music seem to be endless. This section alone outlined reading, singing, physical skills, perception, muscle strength, hearing, and behavior. More may be revealed in future research.

Music Enhances Our Stress-Response Systems

The body has mechanisms that allow music to influence both sympathetic and parasympathetic nervous systems. Each of these critical subsystems (autonomic, immune, and vascular) are vital in the health and learning of students. The basis for this hypothesis, that music can enhance the brain's immune and stress-response system, is the effect of vibration on the human body. The entire body, when in a natural state of rest, vibrates at approximately 8 cycles per second. Our bodies are living oscillators that receive and create vibrations. These are translated through roots of the auditory nerves, which are widely distributed and possess more extensive connections than those of any other nerve in the body (see Figure 2.11).

Music can modulate our body's stress response. In doing so, it strengthens our immune system and enhances our wellness.

Practical Suggestions

In general . . . Music for improved athletic performance can range from instrumentals (e.g., from movies like *Rocky* or *Chariots of Fire*) to vocals (e.g., the soundtracks from the *Superman* movies) or classic guitar instrumentals like "Wild Weekend" (*Tom Shannon Presents . . . The Rockin' Rebels*), *Walk Don't Run* (The Ventures), "Soulful Strut" (Young-Holt Unlimited), "Hawaii Five-0" theme. Don't forget marches like "Triumphal March" (Verdi); Johann Strauss, Jr.'s "Persian March," "Gypsy Baron," "Egyptian March," and "Radetzky March"; and "Rackoczy March" from *Hungarian Rhapsody* (Liszt).

In general . . . Use calming music as part of your overall music library. *Elementary and secondary levels:* piano music (Eric Satie), Bach's *Goldberg Variations* (Glenn Gould), *Music for Airports* (Brian Eno), *Inner Rhythms* (Randy Crafton), and all releases from David Kobialka on violin, Georgia Kelly on harp, and Michael Jones on piano.

Practical Suggestions

In general . . . Students exposed to rhythmic classical and baroque instrumentals (Bach, Vivaldi, and Mozart), showed two changes (vs. controls) in blood flow as measured by heart rate. *Elementary and secondary levels:* To get the adrenaline response, go for high beats-per-minute music: "Shout" (Isley Bros.), "La Bamba" (Richie Valens), "Wear My Hat" (Phil Collins), "Jellyhead" (Crush), Middle-Eastern belly dancing, samba dance tracks, Quad City DJs, Donna Summer CDs, *The Best of Chic* (Chic).

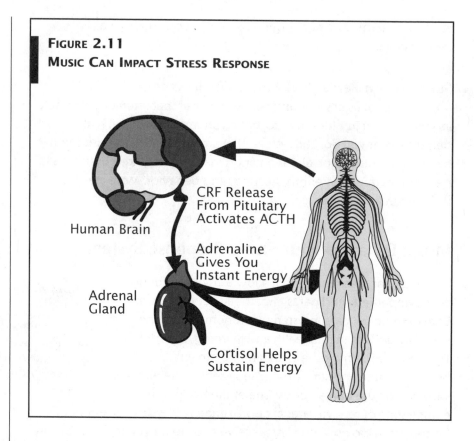

FIGURE 2.11
MUSIC CAN IMPACT STRESS RESPONSE

Human Brain

CRF Release
From Pituitary
Activates ACTH

Adrenaline
Gives You
Instant Energy

Adrenal
Gland

Cortisol Helps
Sustain Energy

Music affects digestion, internal secretions, circulation, nutrition, respiration, and the immune system via these connections. Hence, not a single function of the body escapes being influenced by vibrations. Because the human body is maintained through rhythmic vibration, it follows that a musical manipulation of vibratory rates, changes in harmonic patterns, and arrangements of tonal sequences and rhythmic patterns would affect physical and mental health.

Influencing the Immune System

Given the pace and lifestyle of students, a clear value of music might be stress reduction. Studies show support for the thesis that music can enhance the immune system responses through lowered heart rate, as well as showing increases in parasympathetic activity (McCraty, Atkinson, Rein, & Watkins, 1996). In addition, many scientific studies have shown that music does, in fact, lower the levels of the stress hormone cortisol and increase antibodies in children (see Lane, 1992).

College students were given one of four listening conditions in one study (Newcomer et al., 1999; see also McCraty et al., 1996). One was the radio, another tones and clicks, another was Muzak; and the controls got silence. After 30 minutes, the levels of secretory immunoglobulin A (IgA) were measured. Of the four conditions tested, only Muzak lowered the IgA levels. This strengthening of the immune system can be helpful in two ways. First, many students arrive at school already in a distressed condition, so it can be a brief treatment for some. For others, particularly those who commonly live with suboptimal conditions that predispose one to illness, strengthening the immune system may be especially helpful. If music exposure could regulate cortisol or steroid levels, the value would be tremendous. Estimates range from 3 to 5 percent of school-age children who have some form of depression, depending on their age. Considering that school-age depression is a significant problem, and cortisol is the peptide of negative expectations, it's no wonder so many students turn to music—it's a form of self-medication—it regulates moods!

Music Can Affect Heart Rate

There is evidence that certain music can reduce headaches and relieve back and other postural pains. In a German study, three types of music were used to determine how they affected the subjects. Doppler ultrasound measured heart rate, but other measures such as arterial blood pressure and ACTH and adrenaline were made. They used a rhythmic Strauss waltz; a nonrhythmic piece by a modern composer, Henze; and a highly rhythmic selection by an Indian artist, Ravi Shankar. Of the three, the one with the highest musical predictability was the third, the Ravi Shankar piece. It was the one that reduced cortisol and noradrenaline levels, too (Mockel et al., 1994).

Music Raises Blood Pressure

Music can also raise stress levels. You might like to do that for brief periods if, for example, you have only five minutes left in class and want students to put materials away quickly. In one study, following high-intensity exercise, runners listened to one of two types of music: sedative, fast (Techno-pop), or no music (control). The group of runners who heard the fast music experienced increased levels of stress hormones, whereas the other two conditions showed no rise in cortisol

(Brownley, McMurray, & Hackney, 1995). Evidence suggests there may be a universal response to high beats-per-minute music—stress levels rise! And under certain controlled conditions, that may be good if an adrenaline response is needed.

Summary on Music and the Stress Response

We've learned that music can help regulate and influence blood flow, heart rate, and the strength of the immune system. These effects are critical because most of us have seen an increase in student stress in the last two decades. But school environments are complex environments. We need to understand and influence, when possible, other variables that might contribute to immune system functioning, such as threats, chronic distress, bullying, under-nutrition, lack of physical conditioning, and other experiences that may be out of student control.

Music Can Affect Blood Flow

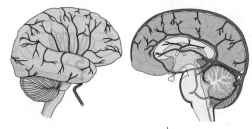

Music Enhances Memory Systems

Hypothesis:

Music enhances the development and maintenance of our brain's memory systems in two ways. First, it activates our attentional systems. What we pay attention to increases our likelihood of remembering it. Second, it activates and strengthens multiple memory systems for both explicit and implicit memory. By activating multiple memory pathways, we can dramatically improve our chances for retention and recall.

Our attentional system is regulated by the interplay of many brain areas. Music can directly affect our attentional system through novelty, volume, catchy lyrics, melodies, a high pitch, and the frequencies absorbed through our bones and skin. Music can also directly influence our attentional system through the more typical ear-to-cochlea and vestibular-to-neural pathways route.

Our memories are influenced by music in many ways. We can encode music as semantic information (a discussion of it or sight reading), episodically (where were you when you heard or produced it), reflexively (an automated music response), or procedurally (the act of learning to play music). Memory typically increased when music is involved (Spitzer, 1999; see Figure 2.12).

Years ago, I was driving to my girlfriend's house for a weekly event, our Saturday night date. But this date was different—it ended before we started. There was an emotional break-up! The long drive home gave me plenty of time to feel sorry for myself. Hoping to find solace on the radio, my fingers froze when one song in particular came on:

Carole King's "It's Too Late, Baby." The combination of the song with the emotional event became forever embedded. But what also became embedded was the *location* of the incident, the feel of the Volkswagen, and the *dialogue* of the story. The trigger to retrieve the entire event is the song. It's powerful because it brings back the whole experience in a way other reminders like a photo could never do.

Music and Memory

The most important cluster of skills essential to musical talent may be a strong melodic memory. Because school success often requires a broad-based memory, it may explain the academic success enjoyed by musicians over nonmusicians. As mentioned earlier, studies suggest that memory is enhanced by music instruction—and the earlier the better. In a college study, 60 students were tested for verbal memory. The ones who had music training before age 12 recalled much more than those who did not (Chan, Ho, & Cheung, 1998; see Figure 2.13).

Music also works to aid our memory because the beat, the melody, and the harmonies serve as "carriers" for the semantic content. That's

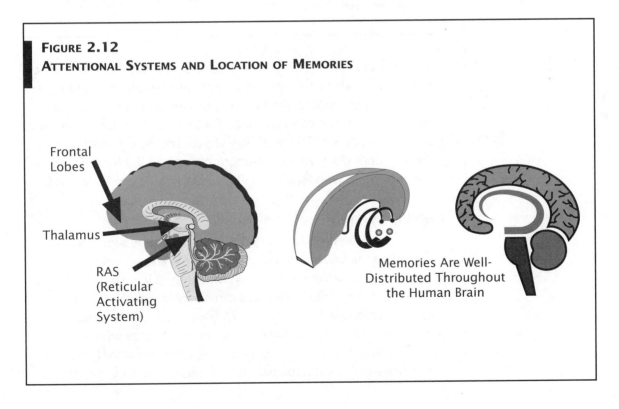

FIGURE 2.12
ATTENTIONAL SYSTEMS AND LOCATION OF MEMORIES

Frontal Lobes

Thalamus

RAS (Reticular Activating System)

Memories Are Well-Distributed Throughout the Human Brain

Practical Suggestions

In general . . . Compile a selection of music that triggers good memories from your school years. Put them on a single tape or CD for easy access. These can be a source of mood regulation for you. In addition, they can serve as memory triggers for the times that went with them. *Elementary and secondary levels:* Ask students to compile "memory music" as a class exercise. Students can discuss what songs or music make them feel calm, inspired, or energetic.

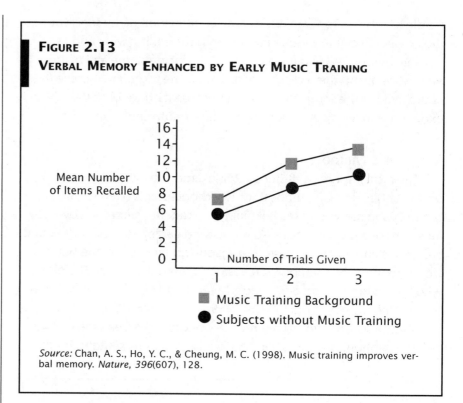

FIGURE 2.13
VERBAL MEMORY ENHANCED BY EARLY MUSIC TRAINING

Mean Number of Items Recalled

Number of Trials Given

■ Music Training Background
● Subjects without Music Training

Source: Chan, A. S., Ho, Y. C., & Cheung, M. C. (1998). Music training improves verbal memory. *Nature, 396*(607), 128.

why it's easier to recall the words to a song than a conversation. Put key words to music, and you will typically get better recall. In one study, at North Texas University, researcher Barbara Stein and her colleagues used two groups. The control group of college students heard no music during their review of 25 vocabulary words. The experimental group heard Handel's *Water Music.* The music group had significantly higher scores than those who listened in silence (Stein, Hardy, & Totten, 1984).

Reading Memory

Music and learning are powerful allies. One study suggests that music aids in the understanding and transfer of knowledge. Music improves the spatial learning in ways that suggest learners may be able to solve related problems. There's a carry-over to reading skills from music instruction (Benson et al., 1997). Twenty-seven kindergartners participated in a program that brought music into their whole-language reading program. Three groups were divided into (1) spoken text rehearsal, (2) song rehearsal of their text only, and (3) spoken and song rehearsal of their text. The test consisted of recalling the text readings, then analyzing for mistakes in substitution and omission. The two groups using music proved far superior to the text-only group (Colwell, 1994). This finding supports the long-standing premise that music facilitates verbal memory.

Musical Arts and Listening

Hearing and listening are different processes:

· *Hearing:* Hearing is simply the ability to receive auditory information through the ear, bones, and skin.
· *Listening:* Music and voice listening require active participation by the listener. Listening is the delicate ability to *filter, analyze,* and *respond to sounds.*

> ### Hypothesis:
>
> Listening training may improve cortical maturation and may enhance social skills, language learning, rehabilitation, and relaxation.

In short, listening is an active and refined skill set, while hearing is a passive experience.

The effect of this knowledge is powerful. What if many learners were hindered not just by poor hearing (as many are), but by poor listening skills? After all, we live in a society where ambient noise is the norm. Consider that a whopping 25 percent of all Americans have hearing loss, and 20 million are regularly exposed to dangerous sound levels (Campbell, 1997). From workplace machinery and freeway traffic to blow dryers, music headphones, and rock concerts, we have become a nation bombarded daily by too much noise. Listening is as important as ever, but increasingly difficult to do in such a noisy environment.

Fortunately, we can actually train our brains to listen, rather than merely hear. The theory that we can enhance our lives by improving listening skills is based on the work of Alfred Tomatis (1996), a French ear, nose, and throat specialist. Tomatis pioneered the use of sound stimulation for listening enhancement. He discovered that a listening program consisting of filtered and unfiltered music and voice received both actively and passively for 60–75 hours changed how the subject's brain heard. The Tomatis Method, as it has become known, trains the ear (auditory system in the brain) until the listener can retain the skills without additional training (Thompson & Andrews, 1999; see Figure 2.14).

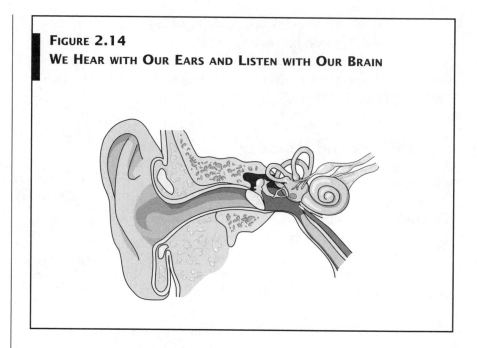

Figure 2.14
We Hear with Our Ears and Listen with Our Brain

The Reorganized Brain

Tomatis (1996) believes that once the ear (hence, our brain) has been trained to listen to music in an active way, as opposed to passively hearing it, a domino effect can take place where other systems in the human body also reorganize. Tomatis says that sound provides an electrical charge that energizes the brain. He has devised an auditory-stimulation process that identifies various dysfunctional physical or motivational systems related to listening, hearing, communicating, and movement, and corrects them via specially filtered classical music, including that of Mozart, as well as selected chants.

Tomatis further discovered that whereas the higher frequencies powered up the brain, low frequency tones discharged mental and physical energy (stress). Tomatis's position is that the ear is a major integrator of the nervous system. Many believe that hyperactive children may be in a constant state of motion as a means of "charging up" their brain. We know that movement stimulates the vestibular system; and this theory would help explain the calming effect music can have on hyperactive children. On the other hand, lethargic students can benefit from music's recharging influence on the nervous system.

How to Implement Musical Arts

You can implement the musical arts in the classroom in many ways. Music can be played, composed, or listened to actively or passively. If you're playing music in a learning environment, remember these things:

· Many students who are having difficulty in school may have listening or hearing problems; and these problems may be affecting their behavior, reading abilities, and attentional patterns. Schools ought to test for *both hearing and listening skills.*

· Making music is better than listening to it. But don't let the lack of a trained music teacher keep your learners from music exposure. Do what you can in the circumstances you have. Everything from humming, to singing, to using primitive to popular instruments, or using CD players can add music to the day.

· Let your students know *why you use* the music you are playing. Help them understand the differences among music that calms, energizes, or inspires. Students of all ages should learn why you use music and be able to suggest selections.

· Always be the last word in music selections. If you think that the suggestions of others are not your style, that's no problem—still use it. But if what students suggest has hurtful lyrics or create an inappropriate mood, say no. That's your responsibility as a professional.

Practical Suggestions

In general . . . Start the learning day with a warm-up consisting of five minutes of vocal toning. This activity can also help disorganized or listless learners. *Elementary level:* Begin by humming in a comfortable pitch for one minute; then move to a minute of "ah" sounds (as if you're yawning). Add a minute of "ee" sounds to stimulate the mind and body. Next, go to the "oh" sounds, allowing your whole upper body to vibrate with your voice. Then sound out all the vowels, starting with the lowest and moving up to the highest, then back down again. These quick voice warm-ups can stimulate the brain, reduce stress, and evoke an optimal learning state. *Secondary level:* Teach students to listen. Quiet the room and ask everyone to listen to the quiet for a moment. After one minute of silence, let students pick up a pen and write down every sound they hear. Another good listening exercise is to ask students to listen carefully to an uplifting music selection, while noting subsequently how many different instruments they heard. Give learners the opportunity to compare their notes with each other; then repeat the exercise. Several weeks later, do the activity again; and this time, have learners compare their prior listening results with the present ones.

• Get students involved in the process of managing the music after you have introduced it. Many are happy to play "disc jockey" for the class, but you'll want to have clear rules on what's done and when.

• Get a CD player. Keep your CDs in a safe, clean binder and keep them and the CD player well secured.

• Do action research with music. Work with another grade-level teacher. Both of you can split your class and trade half the class. You might try one type of music for 10–15 minutes (if it's a math class, you might use Mozart's Sonata for Two Pianos in D Major), and the other teacher might try a series of rhythms or even heavy metal. Then switch the two groups and do a 10-minute exam or survey activity that measures spatial reasoning, logic, or problem-solving. Tally up the scores and share them with students.

• Remember the studies that suggest that students learn and recall better when physiological states are matched. If students learn material with a particular music in the background, they'll also do better with it during the test. This suggests that you might want to use music for learning only when you can match it at test time.

• Approximately 15–25 percent of your students may be highly sensitive to sounds. They may be highly auditory learners. If these students complain about your use of music, you might want to turn it down a bit, listen to their suggestions, and remind them you use music only part of the time, not all the time. At least a quarter of your students dislike teamwork; would you throw that out, too? Be respectful, but stand your ground.

• Background music does affect your students. Thus, (1) select it carefully, (2) make sure it's predictably repetitive, (3) play music in a major key, and (4) use instrumentals, not vocals for the background.

• Some students will complain about music because of another issue: control. If the room's too cold, and students can access the thermostat, they complain less. If the music is not to their taste, and they can have input on what's played or the volume, you'll get fewer complaints. When a student complains, you can be empathic; either turn down the music a bit or allow the student to sit farther from the speakers.

• Remember the power of authority figures and the value of your credibility with music. If you act positive when using music and show that you believe it actually will enhance learning and memory, it will have a stronger effect. In one study, the group that was told music inhibits learning performed worse on a music-enhanced word list and vocabulary quiz than the controls (Forster & Strack, 1998).

· Silence is golden. Anything can be overused or become saturated. Use music selectively and purposely. In most classes, it might be used from 10 to 30 percent of the total learning time. Two exceptions: (1) If music is the whole focus of a class, more may be fine; (2) you may use environmental noise/music like waterfalls, rain forests, or oceans for longer than other selections.

Summary and Policy Implications

The collective wisdom from real-world experience, clinical studies, and research supports the view that music has strong, positive, neurological systemwide effects. There's virtually no evidence of downside risk. So far, the evidence suggests that there are *greater benefits from playing* compared to listening. The enhanced and lasting effects come more from long-term music playing than one-time or short-term music playing.

Schools that have a once-weekly "token" music program for 30 minutes or less are missing the significant benefits, though some meager musical and cultural exposure is better than nothing. The practice sessions for playing music ought to be for a minimum of 30 minutes, up to a maximum of 90 minutes, with a focus on one skill at a time.

It's best to optimize music training with intervals of rest. Longer sessions can work, for one to two hours, if you're alternating short concentrated bursts of music training of 15 minutes at a time, with an activity like dance, drawing, theater, recess, or walks. Students should get this training at least twice weekly. To get lasting benefits, students should continue music lessons and practice for at least one year.

Based on the evidence gathered so far, it's both reasonable and prudent that music should be a significant part of every child's education. It is the ethical, scientific and cultural imperative that all children get exposure to music on an equal basis with every other discipline. Also, children should begin their music education early in their lives, because the effects are greater in the early years. Positive impact increases with each additional year.

Music may be the foundation for later math and science excellence. In Japan, Hungary, and the Netherlands, music instruction is required. In Japan, students attend a minimum of two courses per week in music-making. In Hungary, students attend three music classes a week unless they enroll in the music magnet schools, where they receive music instruction every day. In the Netherlands, music and other arts became mandatory in 1968. Today, students are assigned comprehensive art projects to complete before graduation. The payoff? Math and science scores are near the top in the world.

> The message with music education is, start early, make it mandatory, provide instruction, add choices, and support it throughout a student's education.

■ ■ ■

But it all starts in early education, not as a last-minute cram course in high school. There's no evidence that quickie, short-term Mozart approaches are effective in the long term, especially at the high school level. Use music prudently, with understanding and enthusiasm. That's what leads to dependable results. It can be, literally, an education with music in mind.

3   Visual *Arts*

*T*his chapter outlines the effects of visual arts on the brain and
their influence on student learning. Visual arts are a universal
language, with a symbolic way of representing the world. But
they also allow us to understand other cultures and provide for healthy
emotional expression. Abraham Maslow said, "The arts are far closer to
the core of education than are the more exalted subjects." They can
help construct our meaning—represent our world in ways that cannot
come through linear teaching. The award-winning neurologist Semir
Zeki (1999, p. 94) says, "No theory of aesthetics is likely to be complete,
let alone profound, unless it is based on an understanding of the work-
ings of the brain."

The thesis of this chapter is that the visual arts are an important part
of a brain-based education. They can enhance cognition, emotional
expression, perception, cultural awareness, and aesthetics; they can
play a significant role in the learning process.

What Are the Visual Arts?

The visual arts include design, art production, paper and canvas work,
photography, drawing, illustration, and painting. They also are demonstrated by technical theater work: costume design, make-up, lighting,
props, and scenery. Today many students are using technology as a
visual medium. This includes film-making, video stories, visualizing,
print-making, shooting, editing, and computer-based graphics design.
As well, students use multimedia for art, communication, or marketing

materials and the development of Web sites. Other ways to use the visual arts include architecture, visual thinking, graphic organizers, mindmaps, exploratoriums, and galleries. The questions to be addressed are, What impact does visual art-making have on the brain, if any? and, if the effects are positive, How do we use and enhance these effects?

Typically, visual arts work uses elements of line, tone, color, space, texture, form, value, and shape. Artists use principles such as contrast, balance, harmony, rhythm, exaggeration, movement, emphasis, depth, generalization, pattern, and repetition. Often dismissed as a frill, artistic activity is getting harder to justify as an educational discipline (Sarason, 1990). But, as this chapter reveals, there is no "looking" without activation or creation; and there's no working with the hands without also directing the brain (Wilson, F., 1999). Many areas of the brain and body are engaged to see and create art. In fact, the intricacies of creating a piece of visual art are mind-boggling, which leads us to the brain.

Biological Origins

The human evidence hints that right from the start, humans were making art—as if it were built into our brains. Art-making may have emerged as early as 1.5 million years ago with the arrival of *Homo erectus,* our humanlike ancestors. They used iron oxide pigments for nonutilitarian tasks, showing a clear propensity for art-making behavior. Burial sites showed art-making evidence. Cave painting and early sketching were ways to enhance thinking, serving as a medium for idea manipulation, enhancement, and storage. Art served as a kind of visual sketchpad for thinking—and still does today (Harth, 1999). Another researcher, Ellen Dissanayake (1988, 1992), believes that early art served many other crucial functions. They include parent-child bonding, community building, ritual and tradition embellishment, honoring the dead, and identity formation and strengthening.

Visual art is believed to have taken a significant leap either just before or just after the advent of spoken language. The visual arts may have developed or enhanced the brain functions involved in design, communication, and art-making. Drawing is a tool for expression, complementary to thinking and writing. In fact, art may have originally *accompanied* the spoken word as a form of mental sketchpad. This early form of visual art may have served at least two survival purposes: to provide an outlet for expression and communication and to document the tribe's history. Maybe it wasn't coincidence when Pablo Picasso said, "Painting is just another way of keeping a diary."

From an evolutionary standpoint, any species that is 100 percent instinctive will act fast, but be limited in its responses. One might continually escape dangers, but be unable to figure out why the danger keeps occurring. On the other hand, a species that is 100 percent cognitive would be highly flexible, but sometimes would act too slowly for survival. Imagine having to think through many potential decisions as a heavy object is being thrown at your head. Any cognitive delay may cost you your life. The ideal evolutionary course is to have both: cognition for flexibility, instinct for speed, and intuition to combine the two. But how would one develop and express intuition? Visual arts may be the perfect vehicle to do that. It exercises our creative, intuitive faculties in a way that science, language, or math might never do. Art-making is the realization of our intuition in the physical world.

Developing a Bias to See

As you may have guessed, the total package of all visual arts is a complex mind and brain process. We think most about whatever is meaningful to us. Early cave art depicted food for survival, other tribe members, reproduction, and nature—sun, rain, and water. Although our brain's everyday visual preference is for movement, contrast, and line ends, all the data are embedded in whether the experience may be threatening. The biological and historical functions of the brain are particularly invested in processing moving images, parallel to any approaching predator.

Humans may have developed color vision (vs. black and white in many other species) to identify edible or ripe foods better—such as yellows, pinks, and reds in fruits. One theory is that we developed a four-color vision (blue, green, red, yellow) to make better topological distinctions and, in a way, to solve the four-color map problem. That's the condition of two-dimensional topography, where only four colors are necessary to prevent color-matching boundaries on a map.

Art involves a strong spatial sense, not just a visual one. Howard Gardner (1983, 1999) argues that a spatial sense is a form of intelligence. The impressive applications are in engineering, sports, art, design, and even driving a car. Doing art, Gardner says, is a way of thinking and demonstrating the product of thinking. As a whole, the early expressors of art were doing the same things that we do today: Express yourself, be unique, share your culture, and maybe leave a legacy. Art today is still key to our survival. But how do we create it?

Developmental Periods

Your eyes are not a camera. They are the means through which your brain develops an accurate feedback system based on worldly experience. Two researchers discovered that unless feline eyes have normal exposure to a typical upbringing, the visual system may develop in strange ways. Hubel and Wiesel's (1970) experiments, for which they were awarded the Nobel prize, revealed that when deprived of a world of vertical lines, cats will grow up unable to see them. Their brain, like ours, has a critical period for development. These researchers also discovered how our neurons are organized into columns, which respond to the environment by activating and stimulating neurons. Although it is entirely inappropriate to do experiments like those on humans, the prudent speculation is that our visual system also has both critical and sensitive periods for development. In cats, this initial critical period is within the first three months. This is the time we learn edges, contrast, and lines.

The second critical period is more generalized; it unfolds incrementally over the years. During this time, we learn to see and estimate movement and velocity. We learn to estimate size and distance. This second series of stages is about many areas of visual development, including movement and depth. UCLA psychologist Patricia Greenfield says, "Tell me how old the child is, and I'll tell you how she draws." Six-year-olds copy drawings differently from 3-year-olds and 7-year-olds. Over time, drawers grow from connected objects to hierarchically organized ones, then architectural solutions, and potentially random improvised solutions (Greenfield & Schneider, 1977; see Figure 3.1). The visual cortex has matured as children have plenty of time outdoors, where they can learn, in the real world, how to judge and accurately estimate depth and distances. Some children spend too much time in front of a television. That's not good for developing eyes. They need the experiences that real life affords (Healy, 1994).

Practical Suggestions

Students will want to do art, naturally. Allow your students to doodle, illustrate, and mindmap as the class goes on. Include colors to help make the art a better reflection of student learning. Students can color-code what they learn, as well as draw symbols to recall certain things more easily.

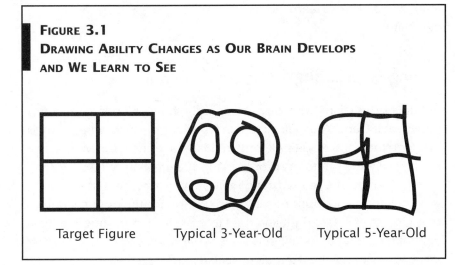

FIGURE 3.1
DRAWING ABILITY CHANGES AS OUR BRAIN DEVELOPS AND WE LEARN TO SEE

| Target Figure | Typical 3-Year-Old | Typical 5-Year-Old |

Some evidence suggests that the benefits are greater when the visual arts are started earlier, suggesting a developmental role in the process (Bezruczko & Schroeder, 1996). As children grow into adolescents, it's time to allow them—*encourage* them—to use space, objects, and their hands. Drawing, organizing, painting, designing, and building all develop important life skills.

George McLean is a professional jeweler, who now teaches other jewelers at the Revere Academy in San Francisco. He said early arts made the difference in his life:

> In school, to sharpen our ability to draw accurately and in perspective, we would design a car for someone (sitting across from him) so that it was right side up when the other person looked at it. It definitely helped develop accuracy in spatial relationships. [After] I became a jeweler . . . I realized how important my art training had been: we had been taught to draw using major arm muscles before the fine motor. . . . [It developed] a lot of patience, a good ability for self-criticism, being happy working alone and really focusing on what I'm doing (McLean, cited in Wilson, F., 1999, p. 143).

By the way, these same skills are often quoted as critical for a wide range of occupations, including dentists, graphic artists, repair persons and neurosurgeons. Once the visual system and its complementary structures have matured (usually by age 14–15), our artistic abilities are

Practical Suggestions

It's best to limit the amount of television that young children watch. Create a good "pro-arts" environment. Provide the following to early learners: (1) enough *time* to express themselves—they'll let you know when they're tired; (2) *safety* to experiment with different media and from the environment; (3) *respect* so that they know their work is important; (4) *interest* so the child wants to continue; and (5) *support* for a wide range of expression.

Practical Suggestions

Make sure your school
has a continuous way
(not a one-shot deal) for
students to actually do art.
It might be building,
drawing, designing, or
painting. The key is to
make sure a student can
do it every day.

ready to go. We can learn more complex visual arts throughout our
entire life.

Seeing Is Creating

Let's follow visual information as it enters the brain. It's got to be energy
between 380 and 760 millimicrons in wavelength—otherwise, it's invisible. First, the light image strikes the retina, a layer-rich structure. At the
first layer are the photoreceptors and the 100+ million cells known as
rods and cones. The retina's ganglion layer contains the cells and pathways that form your optic nerves. Once they reach the optic chiasm,
they cross over (left to right and right to left side) and the information is
transmitted along these millions of electrical wires we call axons to the
thalamus, home of the latergal geniculate nucleus (LGN).

This area in the mid-brain organizes the information based on the
location of the visual input (fovea or peripheral part of your eye) and
the "packaging" needed for where it will be sent to next, the occipital
lobe (see Figure 3.2). Some of the visual information will divert to the

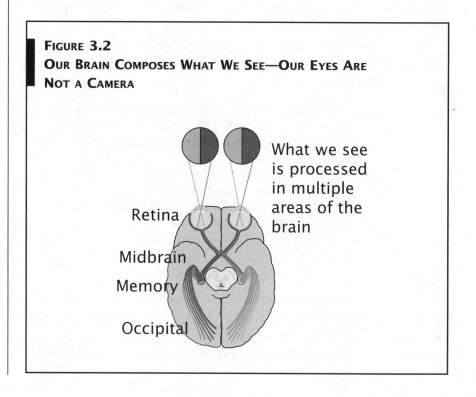

FIGURE 3.2
**OUR BRAIN COMPOSES WHAT WE SEE—OUR EYES ARE
NOT A CAMERA**

temporal or parietal lobes. In general, the parietal lobe processes the spatial layout, the temporal lobes the names and memory, and the occipital lobe processes color, movement, contrast, form, and other critical elements of vision. But the frontal lobes are involved in both the attentional process and the decisions about how long to look at the art. In short, visual art-making and seeing are a whole-brained experience (Barker & Barasi, 1999; Zeki, 1993). Your visual system has more than 35 areas for processing. After all this neural processing, you'd think you'd be able to actually see a work of art.

But this procedure isn't done yet. It's a back-and-forth routine of active input, construction, feedback, and reconstruction. For example, your simplest visual cells respond to the line drawing in the image accompanying this text. You have read the word *brain* many times, so it's likely you saw the line drawing as a brain. But it could also be a mushroom or pool design. If the drawing were more complicated, your brain would turn this visual project over to more complex and eventually hypercomplex cells.

In addition, the brain stores responses to colors. For most of us, pink is calming, red is arousing, blue is productive, and yellow more creative. Seeing anything is an active process! In short, to create a visual image, our brain has to do a lot and *not* do certain things. It's a complex and creative process. Art allows us to learn to see differently, based on what we bring to the table. Pablo Picasso said, "Every child is an artist. The problem is how to remain an artist once he grows up."

As children, we're taught that seeing is all one-way: You see, then sort it out. But that's not what really happens. The brain's visual system runs on highly efficient feedback and feedforward loops (Kosslyn, 1996). These allow you to integrate your prior knowledge, as well as current perceptions into the fast-created image. You are remembering how something "should" look *while* you're seeing it. It's like baking a cake on the run. The reason visual arts are so creative is because your brain won't let you *not* create. Seeing requires developing a created sense of *what is* and *what could be.* Seeing is not a passive process, as once believed. The information flows not just from the outside world, through the retina and optic nerves for processing. It also flows backwards, using our cognition and memory to double-check, mediate, and fill in what we see. That's

Practical Suggestions

Ask students to collect examples of visual art and respond to them using a self-designed rubric or a journal. Students can analyze CD covers or their own clothing for art quality. Students can watch commercials and rate them and discuss the use of art tools such as color, contrast, and motion.

Drawing Allows Our Fertile Imagination to Create Meaning

Practical Suggestions

Students who think they
can't draw, paint, or
design will often try
out a software drawing
program. With technology
as a tool, many students
can learn and develop
visual arts.

why art proponents stress the creative and cognitive side of art: There is
no passivity to seeing or creating. When students draw, paint, or
design, they think and create. Let students know that art is everywhere.

Artist as Neurologist

Visually, our brains are designed to detect patterns, contrast, and
movement. The overall guiding process in visual arts is the search for
the constant, necessary, essential qualities of our visual experiences.
These allow us to enhance not only pattern detection, but a generalized knowledge about the world. In fact, one of the functions of art is as
an extension of the visual brain. But neurologist Zeki goes even further
in his admiration of visual artists:

> I hold the somewhat unusual view that artists are
> neurologists, studying the brain with tools that are
> unique to them and reaching interesting but unspeci-
> fied conclusions about the organization of the brain.
> These conclusions are on canvas (or paper) and are com-
> municated and understood through the visual medium
> (1999, p. 80).

Think about it: Both the artist and the neurologist are attempting to
gain a window on the basic processes of the brain—and how it represents the world.

Seeing is creative in many ways. The brain is constantly challenged
by a series of visual problems. The first is that the image at the retina of
the eye is two dimensional. Therefore, the brain, which is asked to construct a three dimensional world, has countless possible interpretations. It
does this by developing biases as you grow up. You learned that a picture is not reality; it's a flattened, smaller version of it. These biases
become 3-D construction rules. Your brain simply constructs a world that
you see according to a set of rules you learned. If you didn't have rules,
your brain would construct your visual options randomly; and the result
would be flips, distortions, flattening, and other oddities that would
wreak havoc with your sanity. In fact, many of the rules of art are embedded into art software tools. Students can create animated demonstrations
on the computer. Whereas some software programs appear to do almost
too much, many can be partners in the learning process.

No one teaches you the rules for how to see; you simply learn them
from experience. We learn from experience that objects are not smaller
when they're further away. In short, we cannot see distance, we con-

**Creative Seeing
Means We See
A White Box
That's Not There**

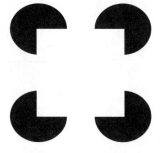

struct the probability that items are farther, based on rules of proportionality in object size. But there's much more. Once we have depth, we have to add to the scene things like color, texture, or movement. All these are added based on our individual experience in the real world. We respond to color in a way that is both gene regulated and experience driven. Visualizing requires both sides of the brain, and image generation is critically dependent on the left as well as the right hemisphere (Posner & Raichle, 1994).

Non-dominant Hands Are Used to Think and Shape Our Learning

Is doing art a right-brained act? Twenty years ago, many said yes. Then, speculation was that drawing too much with the dominant hand would lateralize the brain in its development. There's no evidence of this. In fact, although visual arts are perceived as a unilateral set of skills, the nondominant hand plays a critical complementary (and covert) role. Unlike a static, frozen clamp, the nondominant hand provides plastic, creative stabilization and *does it before the dominant hand takes action* (Wilson, F., 1999).

The brain is sending signals about each hand to the opposite side of the brain. For the right-handed person, the left hand is constantly repositioning the paper or palette *in anticipation* of the right hand's next move. The nondominant hand frames the movement of the dominant hand, shapes the space, provides the buffer, and even acts as counterbalance—all crucial to the success of the task (Guiard, 1987). This activity not only suggests bilateral brain activity during art, but also that the nondominant hand is getting directions ahead of the task.

Express Yourself

The Director of the University of California at La Jolla's Center for Brain and Cognition, V. S. Ramachandran, says a big part of art is its ability to evoke an emotional response (Ramachandran & Hirstein, 1999). When we create or observe good art, it usually feels good. Humans are different from other species: We do art for the mere pleasure of it. Making and observing visual art seems to enhance our ability to elicit and even mediate our emotional responses. The areas most

Practical Suggestions

Give students a drawing assignment, but ask them to work with partners, one sitting across from the other. The drawing student can use only one hand to draw and must leave the other hand under the desk. The other student holds the paper and "frames and supports" the visual medium. Let them go for 3 minutes, then switch. Debrief. What was it like drawing with only your dominant hand? In what ways do we need and use both hands to draw?

We Can Choose To See This Cube Several Ways

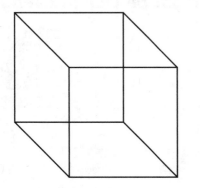

Practical Suggestions

Teach K–12 students how to use visual tools better. Mathematics, a highly visual language, is perfect for student visual art. Students can learn the subject through mindmaps, pictographs, illustrations, model-building, and cartoons. Students can use math to assess proportions for illustrations and murals. They can learn to use estimation in creating yearbooks, self-portraits, decoupage. Teachers are well advised to use visual arts whenever possible to teach all academic areas: graphs, pictures, charts, or works of art—whichever fits best to communicate. A good source is *Visual Tools for Constructing Knowledge* by David Hyerle (1996).

involved in our brains that facilitate this development include the thalamus, amygdala, and reward pathway from the top of the brain stem through to the ventral frontal lobes. What gets the greatest emotional response is both the familiar and the bizarre. Different types of art (e.g., familiar vs. unfamiliar) will activate different areas of the brain. Seeing familiar sights "lights up" *place* cells in the hippocampus. The bizarre arouses our *attentional* system, from the thalamus to the parietal area.

Other art elements create arousal and surprise. For example, symmetry, the discovery of hidden elements, and formation of new meanings also lead to limbic activations. Optical illusions like the Necker Cube (pictured at left) demonstrate that seeing is an active, meaning-making process. Everyone can see lines and boxes. But whether the front facing of the box shown here is nearest you or in the back is up to your brain.

Evidence from skin-conductance responses shows that once something familiar or meaningful has been "uncovered" from art, we are moved (Tranel & Damasio, 1985). While these proposed biological laws probably apply more to design than art, they're a good starting point. No process can stand alone as a link between visual arts and the emotional system, but the evidence hints at a strong emotion-visual brain link.

Visual Arts and Cognition

All areas of the brain are involved in cognition, including the frontal lobes for processing, the occipital lobes for visual input and visualizing, the parietal lobes for sensory sorting, the cerebellum for movement, and the midbrain area for our emotional responses. Of all the effects on cognition, visual arts seem to be strongest when used *as a tool* for academic learning. Studies report strong links between visual learning and improvement in reading and creativity (Eisner, 1998).

If using visual art activates the spatial areas of the brain, then could the reverse work? One researcher used three-dimensional art work and asked students to analyze form, learn viewing skills and develop the necessary vocabulary to respond to sculpture. Pre-and post-surveys were given; exercises also included the standard spatial tasks of object rotation and paper-folding. The results showed a significant increase in spatial visualization skills (Kyle, 1990). "Making art is a highly cognitive process that involves problem-solving, critical thinking and creative thinking," says Professor Edward Sturr of Kansas State University. He adds, "When art is integrated in to the curriculum, the competency scores in other subjects have increased" (cited in Funk, 1992).

Early educational research showed thinking in art was followed by improved thinking in other disciplines (Dewey, 1934). Are your students having memory problems? Sometimes repetition and a new representation of the learning will strengthen the memories. In fact, drawing arts can help establish, diagnose, and retrain memory problems in learners. One way to enhance student vocabulary and writing ability is to use art as the medium for analysis. While learning to critique art, students can increase their vocabulary and language skills. Drawing forces us to visualize and plan our actions. In a recent study, drawing figures helped improve thinking skills and verbal skills in children with learning disabilities (Jing, Yuan, & Liu, 1999).

Visual arts improve reading and math scores. Recently, 96 pupils in eight 1st grade classrooms participated in a study. Four classes were arts-enriched and four were controls with a standard arts curriculum but no special enrichment. After seven months, both the math and the reading scores of the arts-enriched classes were significantly higher than the standard control group. They scored an average of 77 percent at grade level compared to 55 percent at grade level for the control group. The reading scores of the experimental classes, which averaged below the control groups at the beginning, caught up (Gardiner, 1996).

A 3rd grade class found out how well drawing complements the writing and thinking process. Students were asked to read, then draw, think, then read, then draw again. The students found that the drawing enabled them to clarify their ideas better, which improved comprehension and clarity. Of the 14 cases examined, each of them showed improvement with this method (Davidson, 1996). Studies support the thesis that visual thinking using color tools enhanced the cognitive processes (problem-solving, organizing and memory) compared to either using no visual tools or using no color ((Longo, 1999).

Classroom teachers have known for some time that visual tools can help students think. Graphic organizers (particularly mindmapping) can enhance idea generation. In Ontario, Barbara Grandy did action

Practical Suggestions

Give students an assignment to complete only as visual art. They cannot do it in a list or textlike format. It must be drawn, webbed, illustrated, mapped, done as decoupage, or cartooned. Let the students share what they did with their peers, get a peer edit, then revise. Finally, let them share their work with the class, then write down how they felt about it in a learning log or journal.

Visual Thinking Tools

Practical Suggestions

Give students a pretest on a topic. Give a lesson in mindmapping. Now put it into use for two weeks. Each day, ask students to start the day by mapping what they remember from yesterday. They can work with a partner. Then let them send out spies to learn from other maps. Add to their map again. Then do a peer edit of their mindmaps. This process will take 10–15 minutes. Explain to students that it's an experiment. At the end of two weeks, administer the post-test. Compute pre- and post- scores.

research with two groups of 5th graders. The experimental group was given explicit instructions in mindmapping skills, and the other group was the control. Her data analysis showed statistically significant differences in the quantity of ideas generated by the experimental group. The mindmapping group generated 60 percent more ideas in the same time period (Grandy, personal communication, February 5, 1999).

Test Score Correlations

There are some correlations with visual arts and higher college entrance scores. The College Board reports that for the 1999 school year there is a difference between scores of students with visual art coursework versus no-arts coursework. Students with studio, art appreciation and art design (the scores are nearly the same for photography and filmwork) show an average of 47 points higher on the math and 31 points on the verbal portions of the college entrance test. Similar results were obtained for the year 2000 (College Board, 2000;[1] for results of another, similar study, see Figure 3.3).

Fine arts programs are known for fostering commitment to task and social skill development. In addition, many art students report gains in self-discipline, work ethic, and teamwork. This suggests that either being in the arts helps students with the other disciplines, or that only students who are high achievers anyway think the arts are important.

The College Board (1983) says that arts are vital. This organization, which publishes both tests and test preparation materials, knows the value of arts. In its publication, *Academic Preparation for College*, the fine arts are listed *with* English, math, science, social studies, and language. In the opinion of the College Board, they are *as necessary* for college success (and presumably in life) as the other so-called academic subjects.

As one student put it, "When we do art, *we* represents what *we* want to see. When we do science, we only get what someone else wants us to see." Visual arts allow for the expression and release of

---

[1] *Note:* To find information and tables about SAT scores on the Web, go to the College Board's (2000) Web site (http://www.collegeboard.org/prof/), click the "Search" button at the top, and enter "national report" in the box. Then scroll through the items to find the *National Report for College-Bound Seniors* for the years 1998, 1999, and 2000. These scores are also reported by the Music Educators National Conference (http://www.menc.org/information/advocate/sat.html).

FIGURE 3.3
ARTS AFFECT ACHIEVEMENT

(Percentage of Students at above national average)

☐ Control "Non-art" Group
■ Experimental Art group

	Reading	Math Concepts	Problem-Solving
Control	49%	55%	63%
Experimental	49%	73%	71%

One hour per week (music & visual arts)

Source of data: Gardiner, M. (1996). Learning improved by arts training. Scientific Correspondence in *Nature*, *381*(580), 284.

pent-up feelings and validate them in the material world of paper, wood, and canvas. Art gives feelings a form—and an opportunity to manipulate that form. If we feel bad about something, through art we can change the representation of those feelings and, both metaphorically and physically, change those feelings as they're expressed. We want to encourage the expression of art, because it's the expression of our students. And to most effective teachers, what students have to say is important, indeed.

Art also puts us in touch with our own and other people's feelings. We live in a feeling-phobic society. People associate arts with the subjective, hard-to-measure, and affective domain. That, in the eyes of many, leads them to believe art is not concrete, necessary, or real. It's

Practical Suggestions

Use the arts to help students express themselves. Students can make it a daily moment—take 60 seconds and draw their own faces. Later teach students to identify feelings and emotions from drawings.

Practical Suggestions

When there is a compelling event—either positive or negative—at school, ask students to express themselves in a drawing. This is especially good for students at the middle and secondary levels. Events could include a big game coming up, a student who commits suicide, an auto accident, the death of a friend, even a community event. After students draw, let them share their work and feelings with the class if they feel comfortable.

Drawing can enhance perception. Let students work quietly to become educated seers. Students can look at a scene, then draw it. Then compare what they drew with the original scene to see what they caught or left out. Keep a learning log to compare progress over time.

Practical Suggestions

Students could work with information in any class through storytelling, creating a news report about it, or creating a storyboard of the chapter or whole book. The integrated arts approach offers constant mediums of expression for students who ordinarily get little of it. Students are seen as creative, learning problem-solvers instead of discipline problems who won't stay seated.

"fluff," they say. But those naysayers are dead wrong. The evidence suggests that doing art is a highly cognitive process that either prepares learners for future learning or involves them in the moment, depending on the kind of art and the conditions of the learning.

Just as mathematics and spoken words are part of a language, so is the world of visual images. Two researchers call art a language for learning and state that we must all learn it, just like any other subject (Cohen & Gainer, 1995). But it's more than a language of feelings. Cohen and Gainer demonstrate that art is a highly effective way of improving reading, classroom behavior, and the overall quality of learning. British art critic Herbert Read said, "In the end, I do not distinguish between art and science, except as methods. Art is the representation, science is the explanation—of the same reality."

Aesthetic Capabilities Enhanced

Visual arts enhance aesthetic judgment and appreciation of other art. In addition, a study of the arts trains students to have a sense of continuity and a better idea of quality in work. More reflective thinking develops, too. Jerrold Ross, director of the National Arts Research Center, says,

> The arts have a significant impact on academic achievement. Visual arts have the capacity, when used well, to enhance concentration and improve the focused attentional states. They can foster self-motivation and hence, helplessness is decreased. Studies indicate not only that the integration of aesthetics, skill, history and theory, and higher order thinking skills can be applied to learning about the arts, but also that acquiring these skills, knowledge and attitudes can help young people achieve at a greater level in the more traditional academic areas (cited in Sautter, 1994).

Art influences our thinking and memory. In a 15-year research project at the University of Pittsburgh, the effect of visual materials on learners has undergone dizzying scrutiny. Here's what the researchers found: (1) all forms of color are superior to black and white for recall; (2) realistic color is better than unrealistic color for memory tasks; (3) unrealistic color is processed in the right hemisphere, whereas realistic ones (color or black and white) are processed in the left hemisphere; and (4) context does play a role in color processing (Berry, 1991)

Motivation and Self-Discipline

Let's address the issue not of what students *can* do, but what they actually *choose* to do. This is fundamental not only in school, but in life. The areas most involved in our brains that facilitate this development include both the dorsal and ventral areas of the frontal lobes and our emotional systems. These systems regulate how we feel and whether we want to take action on a particular thought. They affect school issues like attendance, school climate, and ultimately the number of dropouts.

Fine arts programs are known for fostering commitment to task and social skill development. In addition, many students who participate in visual arts programs report gains in self-discipline, work ethic, and teamwork. Ask around and you'll find that performing arts are a key factor in reducing dropouts at school. These students will participate rather than drop out as long as you've got all forms of arts including painting, singing in a choir, musical productions, sculpture, dance, ballet, and band.

One student in a low-income, minority school walked into his art teacher's class, looked at his teacher's art and asked him, "How'd you make that?" The teacher allowed him to study arts (though it took special permission). Over the next two years, the student's motivation and grades went up and up. He later enrolled at the University of Pittsburgh. Successful in his career, he now provides inner-city high school kids with an arts education and gives back what his arts teacher gave him—affection, decency, and hope. "My arts teacher saved my life," said Bill Strickland, who, 25 years later, is an architect and now a trustee of the University of Pittsburgh (cited in Terry, 1998, p. 170).

Practical Suggestions

Drawing engages visual perception, enhances eye-hand coordination and creative expression. It allows for the immediacy of cognition to be illustrated in the concrete world. Art is a language, just as speaking or mathematics. That language can be used to express other languages like a foreign language or math. Here are some ways it can be done.

- Concept mapping identifies the micro and macro elements of a topic, and conceptual graphs can help capture expert knowledge.
- Mindmapping can stimulate creativity and enhance recall.
- Clustering groups of similar items can improve comprehension, idea fluency, and organization.
- Webbing helps the learner link prior knowledge to current knowledge

Practical Suggestions

With imagination, you can find a vehicle for expression for every student. Students can learn anatomy by drawing. They can learn English sequencing through the sequences of storyboarding. They can learn history through creating comic strips. If it can be learned, it can be represented.

Visual Arts as an Inclusion Strategy

One of the most powerful benefits of an arts curriculum is the development and sharing of cross-cultural heritage. The arts curriculum enhances teamwork and community-building. And just as important, there's plenty of evidence that engaging learners in the arts can and does reach special populations. Students with disabilities, emotional problems, or cognitive deficits can be served by the arts. In fact, many schools have used art successfully with students with mild retardation (Wiggin, 1962).

What are some possibilities for art? First, throw out all the preconceptions of who can do art and who cannot. Nadia, an autistic child born in Nottingham, England, had virtually no spoken language. Yet by her 3rd birthday, she was producing drawings with astonishing detail and perception. By age 6, her art had remarkable realism with a robust character to it (Frith & Happe, 1994). The amazing sketch of a horse pictured here is a drawing by a 5-year-old autistic child. Though many of her other brain functions are impaired, the visual-spatial areas are enhanced. In fact, the drawing is similar to one by Leonardo da Vinci (see Figure 3.4).

Autistic children are known for attention to detail, but there's more to the lesson than this. Nadia had underdeveloped language, weak cognitive skills, a lack of traditional communication skills, and no artistic training. Yet she produced enviable art. What can she teach us? Artistic prowess has little to do with traditional intelligence, guided by naming, sorting, logic, and memory. This makes a tentative case for the value of art in special education programs. As Gardner (1983, 1999) said, there are many kinds of intelligences.

Children who were labeled as disadvantaged became part of a cross-cultural study of preschoolers. A total of 215 prekindergartners and 228 kindergartners from schools in Tel Aviv, Israel, and Columbus, Ohio, participated in a project to discover the value of visual arts instruction. Some students were merely given drawing tools with no instruction. The others received four-part instruction using (1) discussion, (2) observation, (3) touch, and (4) technical training. The researchers used specialized instruments to assess both the artistic development and cognitive changes. The results were significant, with the experimental groups producing large gains in both countries. The

FIGURE 3.4
INCLUSIVE VISUAL ARTS—DRAWING COMPARISONS

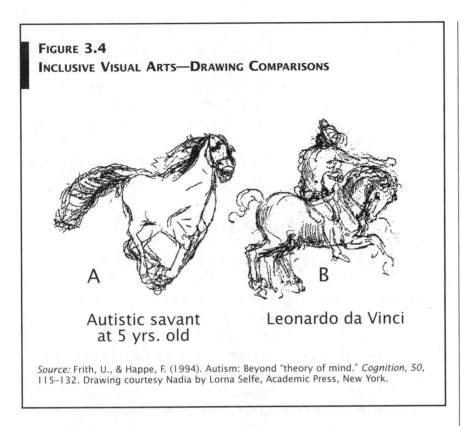

A

B

Autistic savant
at 5 yrs. old

Leonardo da Vinci

Source: Frith, U., & Happe, F. (1994). Autism: Beyond "theory of mind." *Cognition, 50,* 115–132. Drawing courtesy Nadia by Lorna Selfe, Academic Press, New York.

authors concluded that drawing is an effective tool for improving cognition (Mooney & Smilansky, 1973).

Schools often face significant problems in student demotivation; underperforming children are far too common. And certainly many teachers have their hands full, wondering how to meet the needs of a culturally as well as cognitively diverse classroom. Visual arts may be an answer. In an economically depressed area of Los Angeles, one teacher found that by including cultural awareness into the art class, motivation increased. Pre- and post-surveys were done to measure student values and appreciation of alternative art versus traditional Western art. The results suggested that the cultural awareness part of the course significantly improved student learning and awareness (Gomez-Shafer, 1990). Another teacher used written assignments and learning logs as part of the art evaluations. Student attitudes did change over time to become more open minded about alternative art forms. But the surprise was that vocabulary and writing skill increased (Campeau, 1990).

One of the best ways to use the arts to change ways of thinking
about other cultures is to study their art. One school did this by introducing Japanese pottery into a traditional Western art course. The students were given a pre- and post- attitudinal survey that measured
responses towards non-Western art. They were also given a timed writing exam of written art assessment. The length of the students' writing
time increased by 54 percent and their attitudes toward art were
enhanced by exposure to another culture (Fehrs-Rampolla, 1990). Score
one more miracle for the arts.

Visual Arts in the Curriculum

Schools should introduce learners to three aspects of visual art: the
pleasure of it, the functionality of it, and the study of it. The first two
ought to be mandatory. The last ought to be by choice. Though some
people find art history and criticism interesting, most students don't
need to know who did art 30,000 years ago, who did it in the 12th century, or even in the last century. Most students are not concerned about
the philosophy of arts, the statements behind it, or the symmetry of a
beautiful design. And most students don't need to see a thousand slides
in an art class to memorize who painted what and memorize what
school each artist represented. What does make a great deal of sense to
most young people is learning to experience a wide range of art, from
many cultures. Learners not only ought to experience diversity through
art, but gain an insight into their own tastes and character. Formal study
of art and art history can come later—and by choice.

Teaching Visual Arts

The Aesthetic Value of Art

How visual arts is taught is just as important as what is taught. Teach
art as a *joy*. Role model and allow students to experience the pleasure,
surprise, beauty, and joy of art.

· Teachers should bring in examples of art that they like. They might
bring in personal favorites or something found in a magazine.

• Students should be able to share their art with classmates. Peer discussion and student debriefings are good ideas, but not every time. Allow some creative breathing room.

• Teachers ought to make comments about the sheer beauty and joy of visual displays, pictures, and other student work, so that students learn what a source of pleasure the arts can be.

• This joyful experience of art can be done every day (and no less than weekly) by any teacher in any class. It is truly cross curricular.

The Functional Integration of Arts

Visual arts can be taught as visual tools for design, as an organizer, for problem resolution, or as a sketchpad method for learning. Students should do art and experience it, not just listen to teachers talk about it as if it were an abstraction. Participation, modeling, debriefing, and sharing are crucial. Insight and feedback are more important than correction.

• Right from the start, involve students with visual tools. Make sure they get chances to use them creatively.

• Give students choices in using visual tools. One day, they learn through flow charts, another day with a fishbone diagram. There are dozens of choices. See David Hyerle's 1996 book *Visual Tools for Constructing Knowledge.*

• Provide adequate training in using visual tools. A mindmap or graphic organizer is only as good as the instruction and coaching that goes with it. For example, many students try out mindmapping, get little help on it, and either find it useless or too difficult because a teacher fails to provide sufficient interest, follow-up, or variations on its use.

Visual Arts as a Subject

Art as a subject includes the history, the painters, designers, techniques, the styles, periods, politics, community tastes, art criticism, and of course, students doing and reflecting more than they are listening and looking. Schools can offer visual arts as a separate subject as long as they follow a few guidelines:

• The course should be optional unless it's on a pass/fail basis.

• Student interests should drive the class, not a cultural literacy agenda. It's not challenging students' hearts and souls to get tests with questions like "Name three painters who were known for [a particular style] in the early 1800s."

· The course should be taught by a teacher who loves art and is passionate about sharing that feeling.

· The course should be offered every year so that students who find they are not ready for it one year can enjoy it the next.

Final Thoughts and Policy Implications

Research from the studies discussed in this book and the experience of countless classroom educators support the view that visual arts have strong positive cognitive, emotional, social, collaborative, and neurological effects. Plus, there's no evidence of downside risk. It makes sense and is prudent that visual arts be a part of every child's education. Art teachers who have more time with students, with fewer number of days in-between sessions, report better results. Many teachers report better retention, greater student confidence, and more independent thinking. Art vocabularies improve, and greater student relationships are fostered. This results in more focused work and greater in-depth evaluations. What the collected experience of visual art teachers tell us is that when done well, visual arts accomplish many purposes (Cameron, 1992):

· The unlimited possibilities in imagination.
· Greater clarification of self-identity.
· Multiple ways to think, create, and learn.
· The potency of integrity in expression.
· Heightened sense of strength and personal power.
· Greater connection to others and other cultures.
· A deepened sense of faith and mystery of life.
· Stronger compassion for oneself and others.
· An improved capacity to express and illuminate.

Students can use visual arts in every class, every day. Out of a typical six-hour school day, visual arts should be happening a minimum of one-half hour. That amount of time might seem high at first, but it's not. First, a majority of your learners are visual. Those that aren't, need not suffer: the other arts (musical and kinesthetic) will pull them in, too. Second, there's a way the arts can be used in every class. Students might start the day with a graphic organizer or mindmap of the previous day's learning. Prior knowledge is summarized on a large paper. Later this summary can be integrated on a display or posterboard. Or students might develop a plan for a science experiment in a storyboard format. Students can conduct peer reviews through a "gallery walk" process. Students can learn mathematics with illustrations, cartoon figures, and symbols to make it relevant. Finally, at the end of the day, teachers can invite learners to share what they've drawn and why it was meaningful to them.

More and more tasks in the 2000s will become automated. What can't be turned into a computer chip or software program will become highly prized. That includes creativity and emotional expression. You've learned that we do not experience the world exactly the way it is. You construct what you see, what you smell, what you taste, what you hear, and even what you feel (Hoffman, 1998). Nothing is the way it is, without an interpretation. Our brain learns to see, hear, and feel through the experiences we have. In short, our everyday existence depends on the creative interpretation of our brain. The arts facilitate this process more fully than any other discipline. The most valued skills, the talents in highest demand in this new century, will be creativity, imagination, and emotional expression. These are all fostered by the arts. It is truly the discipline of our time.

■ ■ ■

Visual arts represent a way of thinking and expressing oneself. Without this, students are forced to think the way teachers want them to think, reducing creativity and expression. Unless students have access to stimulating arts activities, they're cut off from many ways to perceive

Valuing the Arts

- All educators should consider themselves and their students as artists.
- Arts must be integrated across the curriculum, not segregated.
- Students should be taught and encouraged to use a variety of arts as tool for learning and thinking.
- All students should have opportunity to do art, not just view it.
- Visual arts should be as valued as musical arts and performance arts.
- Students should be exposed to professional artists and art events.

the world. In many ways, the learner is going backward. Although significant time investments are often required to gain potent results from
physical education and music-making, visual arts give you an immediate return with little investment. Art classes are an important feature in
any curriculum, but the greatest payback comes from integrating visual
arts into the curriculum. Estimates are that we receive over 90 percent of
our information visually. When students can't do visual arts, we've shut
off a big part of their world.

4 Kinesthetic *Arts*

*A*s with the other chapters on the arts, the purpose here is not to "prove" that all kinesthetic arts, done by anyone, under any conditions, are a good thing. That's a mistaken position. Instead my purpose is to explore the strengths of kinesthetic arts for student learning and determine how to optimize their potential. The kinesthetic arts play a powerful role as a universal language, with a symbolic way of representing the world. They let us communicate with others, demonstrate human experiences, show insights, and solve common problems. Kinesthetic arts also allow us to better understand other cultures and provide for our health and emotional expression. Movement, dance, physical education, and theater all comprise a different kind of learning—not just different from a lecture, but sometimes better. Kinesthetic arts may enhance cognition, positive attitudes, and confidence; in some cases, kinesthetic arts may grow new brain cells.

The kinesthetic arts can be *dramatic* (dance, drama, mime, theater, musicals), *industrial* (sculpting, auto repair, design, electronics, building, metal or wood working), or *recreational* (recess, classroom games, physical education, sports, active health programs). Howard Gardner (1983, 1999) would refer to them as the bodily-kinesthetic intelligences. The thesis of this chapter is that *when done well*, kinesthetic arts provide a significant vehicle to enhance learning with a huge upside potential and minimal risk. Ultimately they contribute to the development and enhancement of critical neurobiological systems, including cognition, emotions, immune, circulatory, and perceptual-motor. Kinesthetic arts deserve a strong, daily place in the curriculum of every K–12 student.

Where in the Brain?

Movement Enhances Multiple Systems

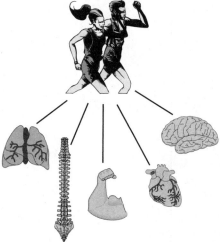

Movement affects the brain in many ways; and most of the brain is activated during physical activity. Remember the old adage that we commonly use only 5–10 percent of our brain? That's out of date. Mark Hallet (1999), chief neurologist of the human motor control section for neurological disorders and stroke at the National Institutes of Health, says that when athletes achieve excellence in a sport, "they are *probably using close to 100% of their brain.*" The brain is a system of systems, and a strong kinesthetic arts program (whether it's recreational, dramatic, or industrial) will activate multiple systems. Using the body means using more of the brain than what we typically use for seatwork.

Imagine someone dribbling a basketball down the court with the intent to score, or someone else performing in a school play. The player or actor would likely engage, at the same time, a dozen or more of the brain's major systems. This complex engagement and, ultimately, enhancement of our innate biological systems is absolutely unheard of in virtually any other discipline. We are always creating an effect that involves our mind, our body, and the environmental stimuli. In fact, there's no doubt that kinesthetic arts activate far more brain areas than traditional seatwork. There are more environmental *constraints to manage* (like other players in a play, the team in sports, or power tools in a workshop) than one would engage when doing simple seatwork.

Explaining the intricacies of at least 12 neurobiological systems for each of the kinesthetic arts (at each skill level, age, and developmental level) is beyond the scope of this chapter. But the interplay among these systems is truly amazing (Gao et al., 1996). Your brain creates movements by sending a deluge of nerve impulses to the appropriate muscles. And each movement, in turn, activates cortical areas. Because each specific muscle has to get the message at a slightly different time, it's a bit like a well-timed explosion conducted by a special-effects team. That amazing brain-body sequence is often referred to as a *spatiotemporal (space-time) pattern or a cerebral code* (Calvin, 1996; see Figure 4.1).

Simple movements like gum-chewing are controlled by basic brain circuits nearest the spinal cord and influence very few systems. More

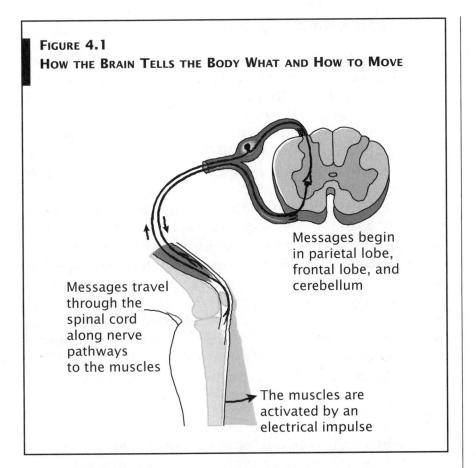

FIGURE 4.1

HOW THE BRAIN TELLS THE BODY WHAT AND HOW TO MOVE

Messages begin
in parietal lobe,
frontal lobe, and
cerebellum

Messages travel
through the
spinal cord
along nerve
pathways
to the muscles

The muscles are
activated by an
electrical impulse

complex movements, like drumming, cutting wood, or running,
engage sequences that are controlled at the other subcortical levels,
like the basil ganglia and cerebellum. But highly complex and novel
movements involve most of the brain. We suddenly must make rapid
decisions, keep our attention up, monitor our emotions, remember our
past, be alert for potential problems, create solutions on the spot, keep
our balance, watch the expression of other faces, move quickly and
gracefully—and somehow still remember the point of the activity. All
these locomotor, manipulative, and cognitive activities are linked with
developmental stages and academic learning at each grade level
(Corso, 1997).

What Is So Different About Kinesthetic Learning?

If you hadn't ridden a bicycle for five years, could you still do it? But if you hadn't heard the name of the capital of Peru for five years, would you still know it? The most likely answers are yes to the bicycle question and no to the capital city question. Why is that? Clearly two distinct types of learning are involved, each with its own opportunities and challenges. One of them has some clear advantages at test time (names of capitals), and another (riding a bicycle) has some clear advantages in other contexts.

Learning is commonly divided into two broad areas. One is explicit, what I call "labeled learning"—what we commonly read, write, and talk about. It includes textbook learning, videos, lecture, pictures, and dialog. The other type is implicit, which includes "hands-on" approaches, more trial-and-error, habits, role plays, life experience, drama, experiential learning, games, and active learning. I call this "unlabeled learning." Researchers believe that implicit learning is, in fact, much more reliable than the old-style classroom education that emphasizes reading textbooks and memorizing facts (Reber, 1993).

As compared to the "talking head" teacher in a traditional classroom, implicit learning shows the following distinctions and advantages (see Figure 4.2). It is

- More robust; the effects are greater, with more duration.
- Age independent; students from pre-K to university level (and well into the senior years) demonstrate the ability to learn and retain implicit knowledge.
- Known for ease of learning; a great deal of implicit learning can happen from role-modeling, nonconscious acquisition, trial and error, experimentation, and peer demonstrations.
- Cross-cultural; this method of learning shows robust effects across the entire range of human cultures.
- Intelligence independent; we learn implicitly in a surprisingly number of ways. Implicit tasks show little concordance with measures of intelligence like an IQ test.

We might want to incorporate more implicit learning into our curriculum. In fact, noted neuroscientist and memory expert Arthur Reber (1993) says, "Unlike contemporary approaches to pedagogy and instruction, the results from the studies on implicit learning suggest that

> **FIGURE 4.2**
> **IMPLICIT LEARNING IS LASTING LEARNING**
>
>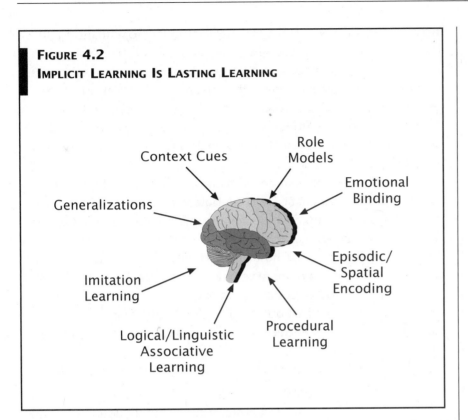

school *curricula should be modified to include more exposure . . .* [and] a tilt towards the kinds of educational programs championed by John Dewey" (see pp. 88–110, 159).

The Role of Dramatic Arts

This section explores the role that dance, drama, directing, choreography, kinesthetic awareness, improvisation, plays, mime, musicals, and other media play in human development. In school dramatic arts programs, teachers rarely expect that students will become professionals at it. The real driving force behind dramatic arts is what it does for the emotional, physical, and cognitive abilities of the student.

Improved Development

Though drama and dramatic play have many direct benefits, one indirect benefit is that it facilitates the maturation of the brain's cortical systems (Allman, 1999). This is especially important for enhancing student learning. Reading, counting, speaking, and problem-solving are all maturation correlated. And it's play that speeds the process. It does it faster and more efficiently than other means because play usually has the recipe for brain growth built in: challenge, novelty, feedback, coherence, and time. Students often do theater and play games precisely because they are *just challenging enough*, with a novel twist here and lots of feedback.

There are some correlations with movement arts and higher college entrance scores. If dramatic arts contribute to cognition, more of such coursework (up to a point) might to lead to higher scores. The College Board reports that for the 1999 school year, there are differences between student scores of those taking dramatic arts versus no dramatic arts. Students with four or more years in dance were 27 points higher, those in drama study 44 points higher, and those with acting or production experience were a whopping 53 points higher than nondramatic arts students on the averaged math and verbal scores (College Board, 2000).[1]

Dance May Enhance Multiple and Lasting Biological Systems

Creativity

In another study, high school students were tested for creativity. The theater students scored significantly higher than nonmusic students; and, as might be expected, music students scored higher on creativity tests than nonmusical students (Hamann, Bovrassa, & Aderman, 1991). One of the activities that both theater and dance students are asked to do is improvise. This may prime the brain for new ideas and the will to carry them out. Rarely is this creative behavior rewarded in a typical pencil-and-paper classroom. Completely untried and novel ideas, however, are more likely to be rewarded in a dramatic arts curriculum or play rehearsal.

---

[1] *Note:* To find information and tables about SAT scores on the Web, go to the College Board's (2000) Web site (http://www.collegeboard.org/prof/), click the "Search" button at the top, and enter "national report" in the box. Then scroll through the items to find the *National Report for College-Bound Seniors* for the years 1998, 1999, and 2000. These scores are also reported by the Music Educators National Conference (http://www.menc.org/information/advocate/sat.html).

Self-concept

Self-concept improves when we gain greater control and mastery over our lives. It improves when we have specialized skills and can get along with our peers. The processes learned in dramatic arts include the ability to express personal ideas without fear or censorship, the beauty of movement, the skills of choreography, and the corresponding vocabulary. Students also learn compositional structure, sequencing, collaboration skills, and interpretation. The qualities of rhythm, coherence, and flow are introduced and refined. Students learn technical skills, including artistic problem-solving, time-space issues, emotional impact, and the logistics of production work. All of these can enhance self-concept.

Improved Learning

The value of movement and theater cannot be overestimated. In the report *Champions of Change* (Fiske, 1999), seven nationwide art studies were analyzed—and reported by the popular press. In one kindergarten class, kids danced their way through the prepositions with the background of rhythms from a Nigerian percussionist. In a 4th grade class, kids created a huge playground map of the United States and literally ran from state to state, learning to identify them by movements. In another part of the study, 10 high schools were offered Shakespeare instruction. The nearly 800 students in the program, almost unanimously, reported that they developed a strong sense of their own capacities. In addition, many said their success with Shakespeare carried over to other complex works of literature, math, and physics (Leroux & Grossman, 1999). In one study in Seattle, Washington, 3rd grade students studied language arts concepts through dance activities. Although the districtwide reading scores showed a decrease of 2 percent, the students involved in the dance activities *boosted* their Metropolitan Achievement Test (MAT) reading scores by 13 percent in six months (Gilbert, 1977).

Vestibular Activation

Dance can develop balance and, ultimately, reading skills. What the developing brain needs for successful movement and cognitive growth is sufficient activation of the motor-cerebellar-vestibular system. Without it, you see problems in learning that include attentional deficits, reading problems, emotional problems, weak memory skills, slow reflex skills, lack of classroom discipline, and impaired or delayed writing skills. The difficulty schools face is that this "golden time" for motor development at ages 2–6 is more likely to be underdeveloped than it is to be normal. We have an increasingly sedentary population. Fortunately, dance routines often include spinning, leaping, crawling, rolling, rocking, pointing, and matching. Lyelle Palmer of Winona State University has documented significant gains in attention and reading from these stimulating activities (Palmer, L., 1980; see Figure 4.3).

Following Directions

A simple request by a teacher turns out to be highly elusive: "Follow directions, please!" Most tasks are actually a series of tasks requiring interplay between attentional systems, cognitive systems, short- and long-term memory systems, perceptual-motor systems, and visual and auditory systems. Dramatic arts can enhance all these systems. In a recent study, children (4- and 5-year-olds) were divided into four

FIGURE 4.3
VESTIBULAR ACTIVATION ENHANCES LEARNING

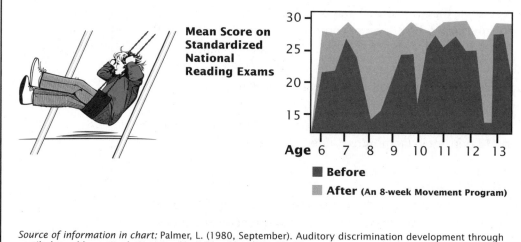

Mean Score on Standardized National Reading Exams

30
25
20
15

Age 6 7 8 9 10 11 12 13

■ **Before**
▨ **After** (An 8-week Movement Program)

Source of information in chart: Palmer, L. (1980, September). Auditory discrimination development through vestibulo-cochlear stimulation. *Academic Therapy, 16*(1), 55–68.

groups: (1) independent study (control group), (2) verbal instructions, (3) verbal instruction plus acting out the related movement, and (4) instructions given in song with music—and movements done in the form of a dance. After 20 days of learning, the assessment given was the Torrence Test of Creative Thinking. The group getting the highest scores were the music and dance group (group 4); and the other experimental groups (2 and 3) beat the control group (group 1), too (Mohanty & Hejmadi, 1992).

Timing

Dancers typically visualize their moves beforehand. One study measured the ability of dancers to re-create music pacing in their head. Remember, dancers commonly do mental rehearsals, both in practice and just before a performance. The reproducibility of these mental performances was astonishingly accurate. Though nondancers were equal to dancers in estimating short (10-second) intervals, in the longer intervals, which included routines from 40-90 seconds, the error rate for dancers was a *remarkable 1 percent or less* compared to a 28-percent error for the nondancers (Michon, 1977). This suggests that the longer the time for mental rehearsals, the greater the success. This example shows only part of how dancers develop and refine intricate brain activations to perform complex movements.

Personal Mastery

Theater and drama allow us to act out our fears, our grief, and aggression. Drama gives us practice in gaining some competence—even *mastery*—over emotions that might otherwise overwhelm us. We are allowed emotional discharge without high risk. It helps us stretch our range of emotional expression, which is healing and stress-reducing. Clearly dramatic arts can play a role in developing emotional intelligence.

Playful Expression

Human studies on playfulness are difficult to conduct: It would be unethical and plausibly dangerous to run a study in which children were raised but unable to play. Further, we cannot make causal assumptions about animals studies and apply them directly to human behavior. Human play, however, fulfills several biological needs (Beyers, 1998):

• Expression of emotions, for enhanced communication and stress reduction.

• Social contact and bonding, as students involved in dramatic arts form lasting friendships.

• New, exploratory learning with challenges, feedback, and joyful satisfaction of success, which activate the brain's reward system.

From Aesop to Grimm, from playing house to ring around the rosey, all games carry messages. If children don't get the messages from play, when will they get it? Playful expression is the link from the inner worlds to the real world. Play is the foundation for creativity. Play is necessary for social skills. Children who are played with, will learn to play. Metaphors and symbolism are created and developed in dramatic arts. The representations of myths and realism are represented through storytelling, with image-rich visuals (Pearce, 1992, p. 155). By age 7, most 2nd graders are ready for the more objective, less dreamy representations of the world. These children need real people doing real things, like games and theater.

Many prominent researchers have suggested that emotional skills may be far more important to a child's success than cognitive skills (see Goleman, 1995). But when teachers feel pressed for time, where can they get these skills? Dramatic arts can facilitate the development of emotional intelligence in children because they meet the criteria for facilitating those essential social and emotional skills. They create face-to-face interactions; and they require managing feelings, expressing verbal and nonverbal requests, delaying gratification, managing self-talk, problem-solving, identifying feelings in others, resolving conflicts, and more. All of these activate the student brain's pleasure center, making arts a genuine source of joy day after day.

Social Skills

Dramatic arts provide a powerful model for developing social skills. Young people have an opportunity to relate with the opposite sex in a nonthreatening setting that includes social discipline and emphasis on courtesy and consideration for others. The close contact of dramatic arts often requires balance, synchronized, and coordinated movements. The entire process of learning how to interact with others in a structured setting provides a set of social markers for acceptable social behavior.

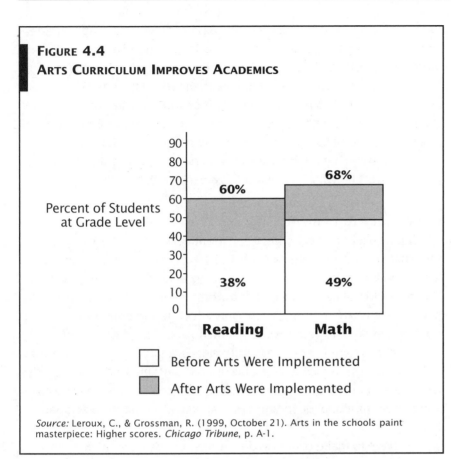

FIGURE 4.4

ARTS CURRICULUM IMPROVES ACADEMICS

Source: Leroux, C., & Grossman, R. (1999, October 21). Arts in the schools paint masterpiece: Higher scores. *Chicago Tribune*, p. A-1.

Cognition

Can dramatic arts increase cognitive skills? While in motion, the brain acts like a flight simulator, constantly inventing, moving mental models to project onto a changing world. This synthesis of proprioception, timing, sequencing, and kinesthetics is an extraordinary mentally complex operation (Berthoz, 2000); and it builds thinking skills.

The neurobiological systems necessary for improved grades include quick thinking, mental model development, task sequencing, memory, self-discipline, problem-solving, and persistence. These and other related skills are developed through dramatic arts (see Darby & Catterall, 1994; Kay & Subotnik, 1994).

Another school was written up by *The Chicago Tribune* (Figure 4.4). At a Chicago elementary school, 84 percent of the students come from families below the poverty line and 30 percent do not speak English.

Before arts were introduced, a measly 38 percent were reading at grade level and 49 percent doing math at grade level. Instead of spending more time on drill and kill in reading and math, the school added the arts. With a strong arts program, things have changed. Sixty percent now read at grade level, and 68 percent do math at or above grade level. *Reading rates have nearly doubled.* Dick Deasy, director of the Arts Education Partnership, said of the study, "People who run our schools have been looking for some hard evidence that what happens in arts classes impacts learning. Well, here it is" (Leroux & Grossman, 1999, p. A-1).

Emotional Attunement

Emotional intelligence has been identified as one of the keys to success in the world (Goleman, 1995). How important is our ability to feel when it comes to learning? It's much greater than you might think. Nature could not have anticipated a world in which information is doubling every 12–16 months, when, only a few generations ago, it was doubling every 250 years. Some system, in addition to the survival of the fittest, has to guide our daily behaviors in a fast-moving world. That system is our *emotional system,* and dramatic arts enhance it. In a study with more than 100 subjects, dramatic arts practice seemed to encourage better emotional decoding in social skills (Boone & Cunningham, 1998).

We have to make countless decisions every day, and it's the emotional system that "weights" the inputs and the meaning-making mechanisms to allow us to make a better decision about whether to learn something. According to Johnston (1999):

> Learning . . . is not a general-purpose mechanism that allows all environmental relationships to be acquired with equal proficiency. Instead it is a constrained mechanism that depends on an affective value system that provides an immediate appraisal (pp. 73–82).

We all have emotions; it's the ability to properly regulate the system that makes or breaks our overall intelligence. The emotions are key to it all.

Movement arts are one of the single best ways to regulate emotions through appropriate expression. A common perception of both children and adolescents is that "the world happens to me." They believe that how they feel and what they believe is all happening to them (vs.

generated by them). As a result, this lessened sense of self-efficacy and empowerment often leads to depression. But students who participate in the movement arts learn that they have control over how they feel. They learn, for example, that dance makes them feel good. They learn that after a walk, they feel better. The feel-good chemicals of noradrenaline and dopamine are running higher in the brain, and that's good for learning and well-being.

Martha Graham said, "There is a vitality, a life force, an energy, a quickening, that is translated through you into action, and because there is only one of you in all time, this expression is unique. And if you block it, it will never exist through any other medium and will be lost." Emotional and physical health is what the movement arts are all about.

Practical Suggestions

- **Use more drama, theater, role-plays.** Get your class used to daily or at least weekly role plays. Have students do charades to review main ideas. Students can organize extemporaneous pantomime to dramatize a key point. Do one-minute commercials adapted from television to advertise upcoming content or review past content.

- **Use dramatic arts as a vehicle.** Mathematics can be learned through building a set for theater. Students design sets and use their math skills to measure, estimate, calculate budgets, order supplies and determine break-even points. Students also master the details of lighting and must learn the physics of wattage, amperage and voltage. They learn weights and counterbalances. They learn timing for music and vocalizations. Maybe most important, they learn to find not one, but several solutions.

- **Get students to dance.** Nelson Neal, president of the National Dance Association, says the biggest thing is making it fun with no embarrassment. He gathers up the kids and asks them to pick any sport, from tennis to basketball. Then he asks them to name some of moves used in that sport and describe them. The students then practice those moves on a dance floor, but either speeded up or slowed down. Then combine the moves from two or three sports and you've got a series of movements that kids seem to like (see Mann, 1999).

- **Support school programs.** Encourage students to get involved in dramatic arts. The theater or dance programs will methodically and joyfully train students in poise, self-discipline, delayed gratification, emotional skills, agility, and personal mastery. These skills can make the difference in students' lives between staying in school and dropping out.

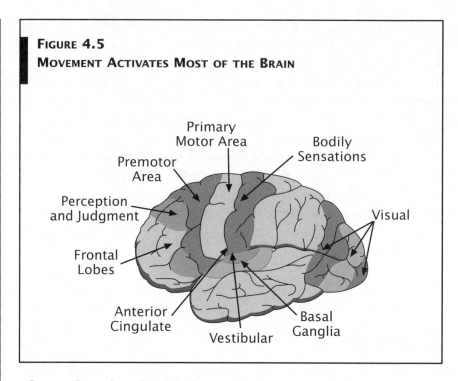

Figure 4.5
Movement Activates Most of the Brain

The Role of Industrial Arts

This section explores the roles played by sculpting, creating displays, woodworking, auto repair, metalworking, and building products out of any medium. There was a time when these "manual arts" were only for the slower kids, those who might end up doing a trade. That attitude is outdated and dead wrong. Industrial art-making does many things for us, including developing the brain and giving us a sense of self-control over our world. Brain activity and working with our hands is so interdependent, so synergistic and complex, that no single brain theory can adequately account for it (see Figure 4.5). The hand speaks to the brain as much as the brain speaks to the hand. With 39 muscles in the hand and forearm, the neural complexity of the simplest movement is staggering.

In his revolutionary book *The Cognitive Neuroscience of Action,* Marc Jeannerod (1997) builds the case that intelligence is not merely a mental phenomenon and that the mind cannot be educated without some participation of the body. This research flies in face of the old-style educational theory. The intricate interplay of our dorsal visual system (traditionally known for its orienteering, but now known to represent the coding of the goal), the ventral visual system (concerned with manipulating and transforming objects), and the temporal lobes (storing and evoking the language of the process) is just part of the process. Breathing, muscle control, posture, heart rate, and countless decisions allow us to learn. The body "frames" the learning context for the mind. It's no longer mind *or* body.

One thing is clear, however, from studies in this arena: Being highly skilled with your hands shows no correlations to academic competency. The reason for it is actually quite simple. Although some children in school move gracefully between languages and representational systems, more commonly, they don't. Working well with your hands is the world of concrete knowledge where something is exactly and only what it is. There's no mistaking a hole for a hammer or a gouge for a beach ball. But school success requires the manipulation of abstract languages like mathematics, text, or spoken words—where the word *phonetic* is not spelled phonetically, math is disconnected from life, and there's no synonym for "thesaurus." For many students, this crazy abstract world has never been connected with the dependable, somatic, real world. Teachers must remember that until you get it, really get it *in your concrete world* that 6 X 6 = 36, it is a meaningless memorization that applies to nothing except a test for most students.

The secret, it seems, comes from taking what we have learned about learning and applying it to the physical disciplines. Neurologist Frank Wilson from the University of California School of Medicine in San Francisco says,

> It does not seem that we have learned yet how to apply systematically to individuals what we know from biology about the nature of human learning. High levels of achievement in purely physical skills follow the same developmental course observed among highly successful mathematicians, sculptors and research scientists. The clear message from biology to educators is this: The most effective techniques for cultivating intelligence aim at uniting (not divorcing) mind and body (Wilson, F., 1999, p. 289; see also Figure 4.6).

Enrichment

The industrial arts provide precisely the circumstances that can enrich the brain. They include exposure to challenging, meaningful,

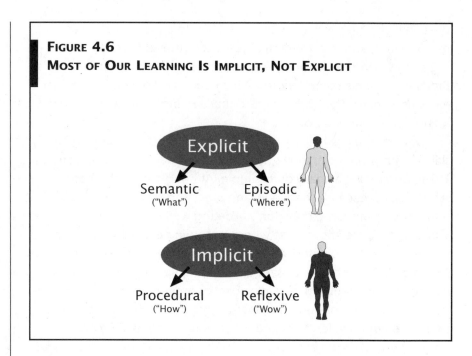

Figure 4.6
Most of Our Learning Is Implicit, Not Explicit

complex, and novel circumstances with feedback built in over time. A project in which the student builds a cabinet, a theater set, or an instrument is good for long-term brain development, as well as self-confidence. The skilled use of the hands and body require countless decisions in the spatial and kinesthetic world. These decision build the same kinds of connections in the brain that we know enrich neural structures. The projects must be challenging, be novel, take some time, be meaningful, and have feedback built in.

Motivation

One of the recent motivational and social problems that has plagued classroom teachers is a demotivated condition called *learned helplessness.* Some research indicates that chronic failure in school can be attributed to this condition (Peterson, Maier, & Seligman, 1993). This condition is a chronic and severe maladaptation to the environment. The most characteristic behaviors of learned helplessness are

• Behavior inertia; inappropriate passivity with the glazed-eyes look, often down and away from the desired focus of attention by a teacher.

· Comments like "Why try?" or "Who cares?"
· Impaired academic achievement.

Teachers who have students like these (from 2 to 10 percent, depending on the school's demographics), know the frustration of working with them.

This demotivating condition has everything to do with inactivity. If you have a student who is unresponsive (depression is an altogether different matter, though meaningful movement can enhance mood), the solutions require positive activity. At school, *meaningful movement* can mean being involved in crafts, design, building, dramatic arts, fixing things, athletics—almost anything where there is active cause and effect. In the classroom, it may mean activities like relays, dance, "Simon Says" games, stretching, playing physical games, drama, improvisation, and theater. All of these movements force an individual to make choices that matter: You fix it or it stays broken, you build it or you never get to own it, you stand or fall, you catch the ball or get hit in the face, you run a race or lose face. This helps to reconnect cause and effect. Next, a teacher needs to ensure that this kind of healing process stays engaged over time; months are better than weeks. To strengthen and accelerate this process, journaling, learning logs, and diaries are excellent, too.

Creativity Enhancement

The creative impulse, a highly personal urge, requires the memory of the past, the willingness to try and test new ideas and evaluation. Working with hands allows each of us to be creative in a way that can show quick and concrete results. We value what we create more that what others create. Mastery can lead to greater self-confidence. Industrial arts are clearly one way to discover an affinity for certain skills and pursue a life of mastery with them (Terr, 1999).

Spatial Skills—Visualization

The ability to visualize accurately is critical in many professions from neurosurgery, to puppetry, to goldsmithing. George McLean's been a jeweler for over 30 years and is quite good at it (see Chapter 3). How did he develop the spatial skills for it?

> I used to build forts when I was eight or nine. I used to like making model airplanes. I would design whatever I was building ahead of time. . . . High school shop

was logical to me. In school, to sharpen our ability to draw accurately and in perspective, we would design a car for someone so that it was right side up when the other person looked at it (cited in Wilson, F., 1999, p. 139).

Using his hands in school, the kinesthetic arts, was the vehicle for McLean, as for many, to train the brain in the spatial skills needed for his career.

I remember reading about a neurosurgeon whose early memories of school included the satisfaction he got from sculpting. Working with his hands and developing a sense of space around the hands turned out to be a critical skill for him later in life. This ability to visualize is not coded by the brain's ability to remember what's in our environment or absolute space. Rather, mental maps are composed of complex motor

Practical Suggestions

• **Use more drama, theater, role-plays.** Get your class used to daily or at least weekly role plays. Have students do charades to review main ideas. Students can organize extemporaneous pantomime to dramatize a key point. Do one-minute commercials adapted from television to advertise upcoming content or review past content.

• **Use dramatic arts as a vehicle.** Mathematics can be learned through building a set for theater. Students design sets and use their math skills to measure, estimate, calculate budgets, order supplies and determine break-even points. Students also master the details of lighting and must learn the physics of wattage, amperage and voltage. They learn weights and counterbalances. They learn timing for music and vocalizations. Maybe most important, they learn to find not one, but several solutions.

• **Get students to dance.** Nelson Neal, president of the National Dance Association, says the biggest thing is making it fun with no embarrassment. He gathers up the kids and asks them to pick any sport, from tennis to basketball. Then he asks them to name some of moves used in that sport and describe them. The students then practice those moves on a dance floor, but either speeded up or slowed down. Then combine the moves from two or three sports and you've got a series of movements that kids seem to like (see Mann, 1999).

• **Support school programs.** Encourage students to get involved in dramatic arts. The theater or dance programs will methodically and joyfully train students in poise, self-discipline, delayed gratification, emotional skills, agility, and personal mastery. These skills can make the difference in students' lives between staying in school and dropping out.

—Continued

schema that are dependent on their position *relative to our body*. We learn and code memories based on our body's *relationship* to the surroundings, not to the static surroundings themselves. It is our relationship with our body's spatial encoding that helps us recall. As an example, when we hold a tool, it's our nondominant hand that shapes the last and next move we make with our dominant hand.

This is one of the fundamental values of working with our hands. It's not just "hands-on," it's "brains-on" learning. It is the brain working with the environment, with our hands. Many other basketball players could play basketball alone in a gym as well as Michael Jordan. But Jordan excelled in the real world through his interaction with the elements in the total environment.

Practical Suggestions—Continued

• **Encourage design and building.** Commonly, children in lower elementary grades will build minicities, plant environments, and pet animal cages. Where traditionally kids on a farm are used to building what they need, in most schools, it's different. Give kids the chance to build and you may develop all kinds of latent talents.

• **Allow students to fix things.** When something breaks in the classroom, or at home, it might not be appropriate for a student to fix it. But it is appropriate at least to discuss it and use it as problem-solving. In some cases, it may work to allow a student to fix something, particularly in an industrial arts class.

• **Encourage sculpture and clay model building.** One neurosurgeon said that he developed his spatial skills from clay work in 1st grade. Often dismissed as childish and basic, sculpture and clay work can be highly valuable; they develop an immense amount of visual-spatial skill. This is particularly valuable when students need to develop other skills like patience and attention to detail.

• **Use kinesthetic models to explain key concepts.** I often use a designer cube based on 24 strips of cardboard stock, each 1" X 4" to show basic mathematical principles. Students learn points, lines, angles, triangles, and cubes all from building this object. How many other objects can be used to explain, for example, photosynthesis, global warming, or communications skills? Remember, don't make speed or efficiency the goal. Let students build them and learn from the *process.*

• **Allow students to build their own tools for working.** Students can make a sanding block, build a stage set for drama, and make the measuring tools for a math class. By building into your curriculum the time and effort necessary for creating the tools, you can allow students to take on a whole new level of ownership for learning.

The Role of Recreational Arts

Recreational arts include activities like recess, classroom breaks, group play, sports, juggling, games, and physical education. This group of disciplines is a powerful strategy for improving emotional and physical health, cognition, social skills, perceptual-motor skills, creativity, and love of learning (for recent information on the effects on learning of physical education and other types of activity, see Caterino & Polak, 1999; Sallis et al., 1997; Shephard, 1996, 1997; Travlos & Marisi, 1995).

Play and the Brain

Is there genuine value of play among humans? In a nutshell, yes. The first reason for it is survival enhancement. Mammals play because it is an activity *that lets us learn without lethal feedback.* Lion cubs play so that they may someday hunt. Zebra colts play to practice avoiding predators. Human games, everything from dodgeball to Barbie doll, and Batman to army man, all have the same elements. First, games are simple, but they grow in complexity. Play lets us act out scenarios in a way that we can learn from them without paying heavy penalties. It's low threat, high feedback, and high fun. Play provides many trials, many chances to learn, low risk, and time to correct mistakes.

From the point of view of learning, you can't beat play. Play maximizes the developmental critical period (up to age 12) during the selectively experience-dependent stage of synaptic elimination (see Figure 4.7). Neural networks, the intricate matrixes of connected neurons, develop by trial and error, where we learn to eliminate poor choices through experience. In other words, we don't become smart by always making the right choice—we become smart by eliminating bad choices. Researchers say, "Playing animals, including humans, are motivated to repeat newly acquired skills in the absence of immediate external goals, thereby increasing the strength of neurological structures underlying these skills and opening opportunities for further learning" (Byers & Walker, 1995). The same games that a 4-year-old is playing—such as jumping over a puddle, skipping rope, and playing make-believe—are later turned into real-world activities. The adolescent, soon-to-be-an-adult, can now play a sport, dodge a skateboard left in the driveway, and mentally rehearse an upcoming conversation with the opposite sex (McCune, 1998).

School play, from peer games to sports, from musical chairs to "new games," may be more important than earlier believed. Surprisingly, play may enhance emotional intelligence by facilitating the encoding and decoding of social signals. In fact two researchers who study this domain have said, "Despite the social consequences of such activity, the mechanisms involved are every bit as 'cognitive' as are those associated with math seatwork, thus expanding the realm of cognitive benefits afforded by physical play" (Bjorkland & Brown, 1998). Types of play at school include

· Exercise play (aerobics, running, chasing, dance routines).
· Rough and tumble play (soccer, basketball, football, wrestling).
· Group/team competitive games, such as relays.
· Exploratory (hide-and-seek, scavenger hunts, make-believe).
· New games (group noncompetitive games like earth ball).
· Individual competitive (marbles, track and field, hopscotch).
· Adventure/confidence play (ropes courses, trust walks).
· Group noncompetitive activities (dance or theater performances).

FIGURE 4.7
COMPLEX, OPTIMIZED LEARNING OCCURS THROUGH THE FORMATION OF NEURAL NETWORKS

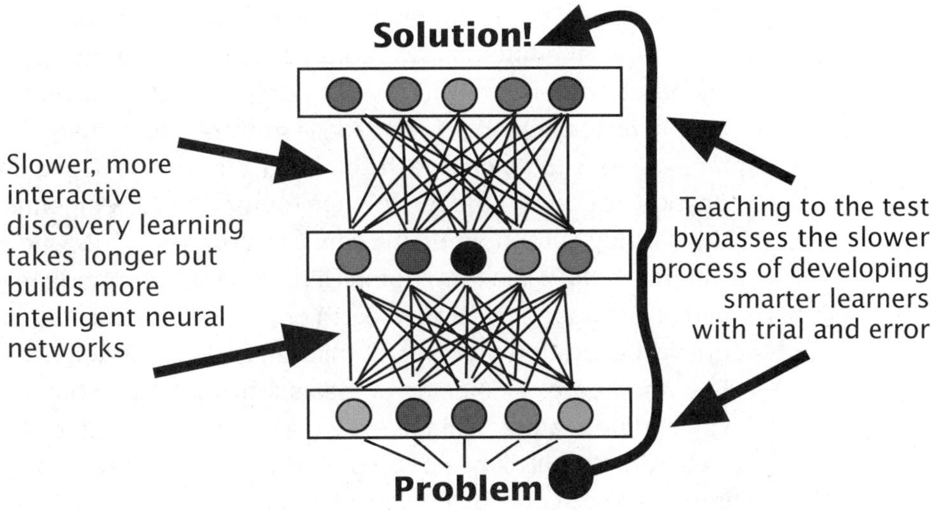

Solution!

Slower, more interactive discovery learning takes longer but builds more intelligent neural networks

Teaching to the test bypasses the slower process of developing smarter learners with trial and error

Problem

Many more children today are coming to school with concerns, problems, and, increasingly, trauma. These emotional issues will either get expressed or impair the learning. Research has shown play therapy to be an excellent vehicle for the expression of emotions. Children with either expressive barriers or significant emotional "baggage" benefit the most from play-acting (Carmichael & Atchinson, 1997). What is it like with no play in one's life? Here's a true story of one person, named Charles.

A psychiatrist had determined that, as a child, Charles never played. He was in the Boy Scouts and served as altar boy, but that was a duty, forced on him by his father. Teachers said he slumped against the wall at recess and never joined in with the other kids. His parents closely controlled and regimented his after-school time. Charles never had time to express his inner world. That is, until August 1, 1966, when he finally expressed himself. On that day, Charles Whitman climbed up and into the clock tower at the University of Texas at Austin and began shooting people with a high-powered rifle. He was stopped almost three hours later, leaving a campus littered with dead and wounded bodies. Play would have been a far healthier alternative for Charles. Maybe he could have expressed his emotions in a nonlethal way. Remember, your students will *always* express themselves, it's just a matter of when and how.

Improved Cognition

Because of the enormous number of variables to control for, the studies that attempt to show a consistent causal link between recreational activity and cognition vary widely (e.g., see Sallis et al., 1999). In the province of Quebec in Canada, a study of 546 primary schoolchildren was done to determine the effects, if any, of one hour a day of physical education. The results were robust. The experimental group significantly outperformed the controls at grades 2, 3, 5, and 6 (Shephard, 1996). In Farmington Hills, Michigan, 1st grade teacher Barry Nofzinger did action research on two groups, the experimental physical education group of 22 children and 21 who were the controls. The Wood Creek Elementary students were ability and grade matched. Pre- and post- attitudinal surveys were given, and the study lasted four weeks. The results suggest that physical education is responsible for improved self-concept, enhanced academics, and enjoying school more. What more could you ask from a program that does that much and costs almost nothing? (Nofzinger, personal communication, June 26, 1999).

Other studies suggest that academic improvement is correlated to physical education (Caterino & Polak, 1999; Dwyer et al., 1996; Shephard, 1997), but we must keep in mind the *big picture* of human development, not just test scores. As an example, the more student-athletes play sports, the more likely they'll gain the positive influence of mentors and social support—even community support. Other data suggest that physical exercise lowers stress, improves circulation, and increases cell growth and growth hormones. In short, exercise may work for many, many reasons. *And there is no downside risk.*

Decision Making

Athletes learn the importance of thinking. Raw athletic ability never ensures success in sports. The best players in every sport use problem-solving skills, split-second decision making, creativity, timing, and risk management to succeed. Most sports are games of assessing variables (perception), calculating chances (the mathematics of risk or rewards), and execution (both body and mind). In fact, the cognitive decisions made by players are what win or lose games more than their ability.

Perceptual-Motor Skills

Can the basic perceptual-motor skills be taught in later years, if the child has not learned them early, during her earlier sensitive periods? The answer seems to be yes, to a degree. These skills include visual acuity, eye-hand coordination, orienting responses, object manipulation, tracing, pointing, and tracking. There are ambiguous links to academic performance when taught after age 6, though there may be other benefits that have not been measured, or may be unmeasurable. Many of the studies that demonstrate the value of perceptual-motor activities among elementary or secondary age learners have inadequate or no experimental controls. However, we know that exercise play may help shape muscle fibers used for adolescent or adult activities (Pelligrini & Smith, 1998b). They may also improve fine motor coordination needed for writing, drawing, reading, and other detail work.

Value of "Settling" Time

Some researchers have suggested that a significant value of recess is that it affords an explicit learning break from the classroom-style cognitive tasks. But recess is still an opportunity for important work inside the brain. A break from academics is what enhances academics because time invested in *not learning* (no new input) is actually essential to the learning process, because the brain cannot organize, codify, and store an unlimited amount of new material in a short time. The hippocampus, acting as the brain's "surge protector," is easily overloaded. Once the explicit information has been taken in by the hippocampus for processing, it continually presents information to the cortex in micro bits, not truckloads. It functions best with a steady stream of micro information packages, with pauses for processing, like recess. Give students small chunks of information, processing time, then a rest from the material. This allows the neurons to better "wire together" for longer-lasting memory formation (Spitzer, 1999).

Too much new learning, too fast, integrated into our more long-term systems would create catastrophic oscillations, neural instability, and unstructured widespread change (McClelland & McNaughton, 1995). In fact, according to M. A. Wilson and McNaughton (1994), we need recess so much that our brain takes an additional "recess" at night during sleep time to process our learning from the day before. Our brain has its limitations, particularly with the high levels of novelty in the world of children. "Young children in particular may require more breaks from seatwork and more frequent changes in activities" (Bjorkland & Brown, 1998).

What happens in schools where there are frequent breaks from seatwork? Not surprisingly, academic achievement goes up. It is commonly believed that most schools in Japan and Taiwan are producing higher test scores in most disciplines, supposedly a reflection on academic rigor. But is that the real reason? First graders in Taipei (Taiwan) and Sendai (Japan) actually spend fewer hours in school than 1st graders in, say, Minneapolis, Minnesota (Stevenson & Lee, 1990). But the thinking of the educators seems to be far more brain based: Their instruction is more intensive, followed by twice as many recesses and shorter school days for the youngest children. This allows for more socialization, music lessons, and peer play at home.

Health

The President's Council on Physical Fitness and Sports (see U.S. Department of Health and Human Services, 1996, 1999) recommends that every school-age child get at least 30 minutes a day of physical education. But only 36 percent of children get that, and one study shows close to half (over 40 percent) of 5-year-olds have at least one heart disease risk factor from obesity or diet. Quality physical education programs, ones that are taught by trained specialists play a significant role in the mental, emotional and physical health of our children (Seefelt & Vogel, 1986). The pleasant experiences students have in recreational arts may stimulate the immune system for several days. Better yet, having fun can reinforce that school is a good place to be. Keeping students in school may be one of the greatest benefits of all.

The Value of Activity

Though we *can* learn while sitting, it turns out that the typical notion of sitting in chairs for an extended time may be misguided. The human body, for the last thousand generations, has primarily been walking, sleeping, leaning, running, doing, or squatting. As Howard Gardner (1999) stated,

> I believe in action and activity. The brain learns best and retains most when the organism is actively involved in exploring physical sites and materials and asking questions to which it actually craves answers. Merely passive experiences tend to attenuate and have little lasting impact" (p. 82).

The body has not adapted to the chair. Sitting is hard work and bad ergonomics (see Figure 4.8). The typical student who is sitting much of the day runs the following risks:

- Poor breathing.
- Strained spinal column and lower back nerves.
- Overall body fatigue.
- Less opportunity for implicit learning.

"Sitting in any chair for more than a short (ten minute) interval is likely to have negative effects on your physical self, hence your mental

Practical Suggestions

• Teachers need to engage students in a greater variety of postures, including reclining, leaning, perching, or even squatting.

• We must engage learners in far more activity (recreational, industrial, or dramatic) as part of the learning process. Teachers should use far more games, energizers, paired and group stretching, and walking. The Director of the Institute of Occupational Health in Milan, Italy, said, "Holding *any* posture for long periods of time is the ultimate problem; but holding the classic right-angle seated posture in particular has its special stresses, *which no amount of ergonomic tinkering can eliminate*" (Grieco, 1986, p. 345).

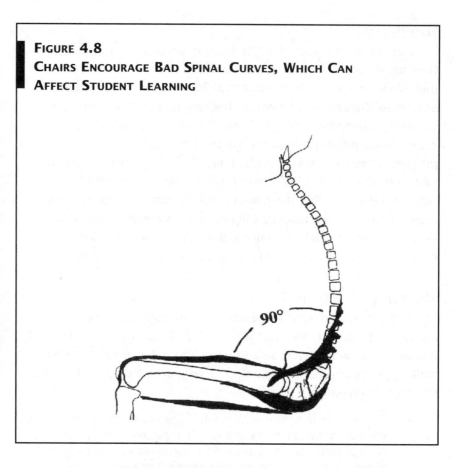

FIGURE 4.8
CHAIRS ENCOURAGE BAD SPINAL CURVES, WHICH CAN AFFECT STUDENT LEARNING

self, and at a minimum, reduce your awareness of physical and emotional sensations" (Cranz, 1998). The pressure on the spinal discs is 30 percent greater when sitting than when standing ("Sitting Down on the Job," 1981; Zacharkow, 1988). That creates fatigue, which is bad for learning. Students get restless and become unable to concentrate or they often become discipline problems.

It's now known that today's chairs do not offer enough flexibility to optimize learning (Tittle & Webber, 1973). As far back as 1912, Maria Montessori described the impact of introducing chairs to school: "Children were not disciplined, but annihilated" (Benton, 1986, p. 787). Though the height of children has been increasing over the past few decades, chairs have been shrinking. Keep in mind, children's visual focus distance is less than that of adults, averaging 12 inches. As a result, they compensate by leaning over, rounding their backs and creating strain. Students need slanted desks, rolled front seat edges, and foot rests. Realistically, investing in quality chairs for students won't happen. The alternative is teachers who understand the value of movement as a part of the learning process.

Auditory Discrimination

Surprisingly, we build auditory discrimination when we engage our learners in rolling, tumbling, and spinning activities (L. Palmer, 1980; note that this researcher has a new study in progress). Our brain does that because those activities stimulate the vestibulo-cochlear areas, which are connected by the eighth cranial nerve to sensory receptors, the cerebellum and ultimately, both hemispheres. Results from kindergarten and remedial learning settings suggest that sensory stimulation affected all learners, but those with the least deficits made the most progress. There was no differences noted in age. While these activities are not appropriate for adolescent and adult learners, they do make sense for younger students.

Self-esteem

Can movement activities enhance self-esteem? Of particular interest is the group of students who are normally most at-risk for low self-esteem. These include those from low socioeconomic backgrounds and those with learning disabilities, emotional problems, and physical impairments. This group was the one that began to feel more important and valued when involved in physical activities (Gerber, 1996; Burton et al., 1999, in *Champions of Change*). Researchers hypothesize about the probable effects of physical activity on the brain. Gross motor movements, like walking or swimming, increase dopamine production, one of the brains' reward chemicals. The most likely effects are an immediate increase of the feel-good chemicals like dopamine, plus an increase of adrenaline and endorphins. Exercise is known to modulate the body's levels of serotonin, our mood stabilizer. The secondary effects occur when one gains more control and even mastery over one's body. This can stimulate the body's production of endorphins (Pert, 1997).

A meta-analysis shows more than 100 articles that link physical education and self-esteem. Of those, about one-third have sufficient quality of data to show that physical education significantly affects how we feel about ourselves. Children in physical education or in directed play exceed the self-esteem scores of those who are not. The physical fitness programs with clear objectives and good follow-through were singled out as particularly beneficial (see Burton et al., 1999).

Value of Daylight

Over the past 50 years, school time has meant more time in darker environments. Lifestyle and safety concerns mean that fewer children walk to school. Ignorance and budget constraints translate to less school lighting, both artificial and natural. This could be a big problem. Present only in the outdoors, ultraviolet light activates the synthesis of vitamin D, which aids in the absorption of essential minerals, such as calcium. Sufficient mineral intake, including calcium, is essential for proper cognition.

Many experts think children suffer from poor illumination at school. A large study from the Heschong Mahone Consulting Group in Sacramento, California, verified this—and caught the eye of the popular press. Researchers examining light and productivity studied 21,000 students in three states for academic performance. Every single classroom was rated from 1 to 6 based on how much illumination students received. The daylight, not direct sunlight, is what students benefited from the most. Students in the brightest classrooms (better skylights and more natural lighting) scored 20–25 percent higher on reading and math scores than did students in the poorly lit classrooms. Researchers are not yet sure how to account for this difference, though they suspect that the light regulates mood, hormones, and visual acuity (Heschong Mahone, 1999; see also Cooper, 1999; see Figure 4.9).

Motivation

The neural mechanisms for exercise and motivation are probably very simple. First, if you already like exercise, doing it provides pleasure. Second, you may benefit from an increase in catecholamines (norepinephrine, dopamine, etc.), which typically serve to energize and elevate mood. Hence, the motivation from physical education may be an activation of the noradrenergic system.

If you increase the time children spend on physical education, will academic scores go up or down? Apparently they go up. Vanves is a suburb of Paris and home of the first school to try radical experiments with physical education and movement in their curriculum. In the

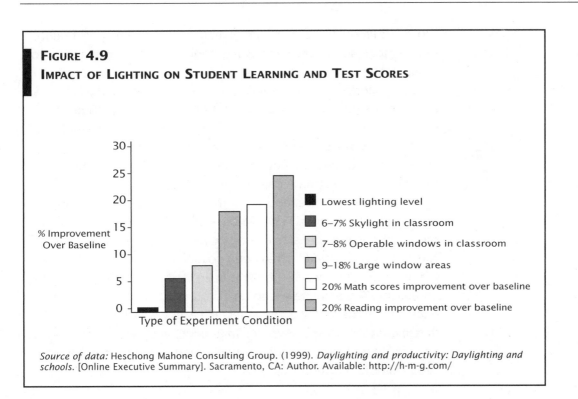

FIGURE 4.9

IMPACT OF LIGHTING ON STUDENT LEARNING AND TEST SCORES

% Improvement Over Baseline

Type of Experiment Condition

- Lowest lighting level
- 6–7% Skylight in classroom
- 7–8% Operable windows in classroom
- 9–18% Large window areas
- 20% Math scores improvement over baseline
- 20% Reading improvement over baseline

Source of data: Heschong Mahone Consulting Group. (1999). *Daylighting and productivity: Daylighting and schools.* [Online Executive Summary]. Sacramento, CA: Author. Available: http://h-m-g.com/

1950s, community leaders were concerned school was becoming too much bookwork and not active enough. The researchers designed a 10-year experiment and selected a portion of the students for a special program. This experimental group was allocated one-third of their time for physical education and two-thirds for more sedate learning. After 10 years, researchers compared the control and experimental groups in both *affective* and *academic* achievement. Students in the "extra physical education" group were healthier, happier, had fewer discipline problems, and were equal to or better than the other students in all academic areas (Martens, 1982).

Social Skills

One study showed how physical activity can influence moral reasoning. Students were selected from 4th to 6th grades, 452 in total. The three test groups were (1) control, (2) a separate "Fair Play for Kids" curriculum taught during the regular physical education time, and (3) "Fair Play for Kids" integrated across the curriculum. The experiment ran for seven months, and researchers used moral development indicators

(Horrock's Prosocial Play Behavior Inventory) for pre- and post-testing. Fair Play for Kids is a teacher resource manual and interdisciplinary program that focuses on moral development. The results showed that the children's moral reasoning skills improved significantly in the two experimental groups, but that the control group's did not (Gibbons, Ebbeck, & Weiss, 1995). In this study, the physical education—only and integrated approach were equal in their effectiveness.

Physical exercise can reduce aggression, but only when the activities are noncompetitive. A daily regimen of jogging, weightlifting, and other activities of choice reduced both verbal aggression and anger in prison inmates (Wagner, 1997). Another study found that movement therapy reduced aggression among boys in a long-term psychiatric care unit (Mosseri, 1998). It has been documented for decades that highly competitive activities contribute to increases in testosterone and adrenaline. The point here is not to discourage any competition, but to encourage some follow-up activities (like walks, stretching, or yoga) that might calm down the system. In general, studies commonly report better social skills and cognition when engaged in daily physical education (Biddle & Armstrong, 1992).

Stress Reduction

Chronic stress releases excess cortisol, which may kill neurons in the hippocampus, a critical area of the brain needed for long-term memory formation. Studies suggest that exercise can reduce stress. Although the exact mechanisms for this amelioration are unknown, exercise prevents stress-induced tissue catecholamine depletion. It's likely that exercise does a double whammy on stress—it blunts our response to it and triggers the release of norepinephrine, which provides energy to stay active and focused.

If stress were reduced, would the subjects perform better? A study at Scripps College in Claremont, California, tested 124 people who were divided equally into exercisers and nonexercisers. Those who exercised 75 minutes a week demonstrated quicker reactions, thought better, and remembered more (Michaud & Wild, 1991; see Figure 4.10).

Working out your body conditions your brain to respond to challenges quickly. Moderate amounts of exercise, three times a week, 20 minutes a day, can ensure that the stress-reduction benefits happen. It also helps learners better manage their blood pressure (Bazzano et al.,

FIGURE 4.10
EXERCISE IMPROVES THE STRESS RESPONSE

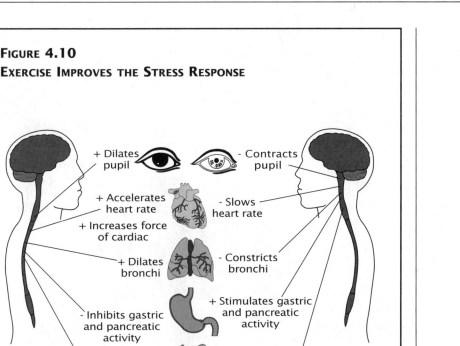

+ Dilates pupil

- Contracts pupil

+ Accelerates heart rate

- Slows heart rate

+ Increases force of cardiac

+ Dilates bronchi

- Constricts bronchi

- Inhibits gastric and pancreatic activity

+ Stimulates gastric and pancreatic activity

- Inhibits GI activity

+ Stimulates GI motility and secretion

1992). This regulation can lead to better social skills and reduced discipline problems.

When teachers complain that students are not in a good state to learn, they should consider movement. Robert Thayer, who has researched the influence of movement on mood regulation for 20 years, is adamant about the power of movement. He says, "The data suggests that exercise is the best overall mood regulator" (1996, p. 128). Teachers who have learners sit too long, from pre-K through the college years, are missing the boat. Thayer suggests, aside from mandated vigorous exercise, that going for brisk walks is the single best way teachers can influence student's moods. A consistent physical education program not only puts students in better moods, but generally improves achievement.

Neurogenesis

Research has revealed what may be the ultimate benefits of exercise: new brain cells. For the past 100 years, one of the so-called

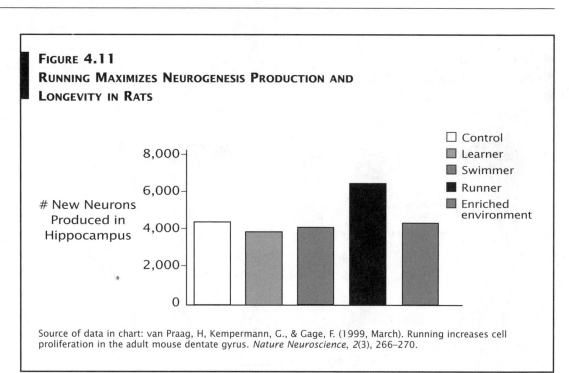

FIGURE 4.11
RUNNING MAXIMIZES NEUROGENESIS PRODUCTION AND LONGEVITY IN RATS

Source of data in chart: van Praag, H, Kempermann, G., & Gage, F. (1999, March). Running increases cell proliferation in the adult mouse dentate gyrus. *Nature Neuroscience, 2*(3), 266–270.

immutable laws of brain science was that the human brain cannot grow new cells (neurogenesis). This dogma was shattered by the work of Fred Gage and his team from The Salk Institute in La Jolla, California. The exciting new discoveries in neurogenesis tell us that humans can and do grow new brain cells daily. To discover what enhances new neuron growth, Gage's colleague, Henriette van Praag, used rats with four different experimental conditions. She discovered that running (versus swimming, learning, control, or enriched environment) is the top brain-cell producer (van Praag, Kempermann, & Gage, 1999; see Figure 4.11). Moreover, four weeks later, more of the new neurons survived (from running) and became functional. While we await studies on humans, if you needed a good excuse to exercise, gaining new neurons may be as good as it gets.

Summary and Policy Implications

Here's the bottom line on the kinesthetic arts: The research, the theory, and real-world classroom experience clearly support sustaining or increasing the role of movement in learning. Movement has strong positive cognitive, emotional, social, collaborative, and neurological

Practical Suggestions

• **Support physical education.** Use flexibility and conditioning programs with purposeful goals. Engage students in "new games" often, where there is no losing and everyone wins. Ensure that the programs are daily so students feel the benefits and miss it when they're away from it. Add celebrations to keep it fun. Design activities that include everyone, not just the better athletes. The best studies suggest that daily physical exertion of 30–40 minutes will maximize the many dormant potentials in learners.

• **Less sitting.** Nearly every activity done in schools that is done sitting, can be done standing, leaning, squatting, walking, or lying down. Educators have got to consider the strong influence the body has on the brain. An active classroom environment will enhance learning and make it a priority (as opposed to *control* as the priority). Teachers should regularly engage students in far more movement. And they should fight for more ergonomic furniture and take advantage of a larger variety of postures, including leaning, perching, lying down, or standing. The typical classroom full of kids sitting slumped in bad chairs is ludicrous considering what we now know about movement, chairs, and learning.

• **Energizers.** Here are just a few: Use the body to measure things around the room and report the results: "This cabinet is 99 knuckles long." Play a "Simon Says" game with content built into the game: "Simon says point to the South. Simon says point to three different sources of weather information in this room." Do team jigsaw processes with huge, poster-sized mindmaps. Get up and touch around the room seven colors in order on seven different objects. Teach a move-around system using memory cue words. "Stand in the room where we first learned about such and such (see Griss 1994)."

• **Active games.** Ball-toss games can be used as review, for vocabulary-building, storytelling, or self-disclosure. Students can rewrite lyrics to familiar songs in pairs or on a team. The new words are a content review. Then they perform it with choreography. Get physical, too. Play a tug-of-war game where everyone gets a partner and picks a topic from the list that all have been learning about. Each person has his own opinion about the topic. The goal is to convince their partner in a 30-second argument why their topic is more important. After the verbal combat, the issue has to be settled physically with a giant tug of war. All partners are on opposite sides. See *Minds in Motion* by Susan Griss (1998).

• **Cross-laterals.** Learn and use arm and leg cross-over activities that can force both of the brain's hemispheres to "talk" to each other better. "Pat your head and rub your belly" is an example of a cross-over. These include marching in place while patting opposite knees, patting yourself on the opposite shoulder and touching opposite elbows or heels. Several books, including *Brain Gym, Teachers Edition* by Paul and Gail Dennison (1989) and *Smart Moves* by Carla Hannaford (1995), have these activities.

• **Stretching.** To open the class, or anytime that you need some more energy, get everyone up to do some slow stretching. Ask students to lead the group as a whole or let teams do their own stretching, and rotate stretching leaders. Allow learners more mobility in the classroom during specific times. Have errands they can do, keep a jump rope available, or simply let students walk around the back of the room as long as they avoid disturbing other students.

effects. There is considerable potential for upside gain both from the physical and nonphysical spin-offs. It makes strong sense that a variety of movement activities should support and sustain every child's education. In fact, it is our ethical, scientific, and health imperative that all children get mandated exposure to the movement arts.

A meager 36 percent of K–12 students in the United States participate in a daily physical education program. An astonishingly low 49 of 50 states have no mandated physical education curriculum for all students at all levels. The only state with mandated K–12 physical education is Illinois; and only Alabama and Washington state have mandated physical education for the K–8 level. We are in a time when most children don't participate in physical education. But when done well, physical education is meaningful, inclusive, energizing, challenging, and consistent. Remove any of those qualities and you'll have students who would rather not participate. Ensure that all those factors are present, and you'll have students begging to participate.

Budget cuts often target the arts and physical education as "frills." That's a shame because there's good evidence that these activities are not only what makes school interesting to many students, but what also can help boost academic performance. Evidence suggests that the grade point average of both boys and girls actually goes up *while participating* in sports, not down (Silliker & Quirk, 1997). Participation in fine arts decreases the chances a student will drop out by 15 percent. That alone sounds good, but participation in school athletics decreases dropout probability by a whopping 40 percent (McNeal, 1995). Research suggests that extracurricular activities are positively correlated with improved relationships, greater motivation, and academic improvement (see Burton et al., 1999).

■   ■   ■

Years ago, the arts magnet schools were getting all the press and attracting many inner-city kids. Today, it's the savvy schools that are making movement arts a priority. When schools report problems with recess, physical education classes, and other kinesthetic curriculum, they ought to fix the problem, not throw out activity. Some programs need better planning; others need more meaning, choice, and purpose. Some programs need goals and supervision, too. But regardless of that they need, it makes more sense to fix an ailing program than to get rid of it. Many studies suggest that physical activity provides a slew of benefits that are well worth the investment (e.g., Caterino & Polak, 1999; Shephard, 1997). If you're looking for miracles, look no further. There is also a clear mandate for the implementation of programs early on, because the effects are greater in the early years. Having said that, it is essential that the kinesthetic arts be mandatory throughout the learner's education. There is simply too much to gain and too little to lose. It's time to get moving and put movement back in the curriculum.

5   *Arts* and Assessment

*I*f you accept the value of arts, then the assessment issue follows. Either arts should be assessed or should not be assessed. The decisions about assessment will affect public perception of the arts; student learning; and, ultimately, local, state, and federal support for the arts. The purpose of this chapter is to illuminate the pertinent issues and make recommendations on the issue of assessing arts.

Assessment Questions

There are really only three questions regarding arts and assessment. The first is, "Can we?" The second is, "Should we?" The third is, "If we should, how?" The answer to the first question is a clear yes. Many dedicated educators have developed clear guidelines for assessing the arts (e.g., Armstrong, 1994; Burz & Marshall, 1999; Wisconsin Department of Public Instruction, 1997[1]). These guidelines are at least on par with any developed for the so- called "hard" disciplines of science, math, or languages.

    The second question, "Should we?" is a bit more difficult. The thesis of this book is that art-making develops many essential neurobiological systems. The difficulty with this is that you cannot directly measure *any* complex system. You can't easily measure global warming, the Space program, or a collection of complex bodily systems. Teaching arts

---

[1]To access information about Wisconsin's Model Academic Standards for Arts, visit the department's Publications Catalog (http://www.dpi.state.wi.us/dpi/dltcl/eis/pubsales/arts.html) and discover low-cost publications available on "A Guide to Curriculum Planning in . . . Art Education, Classroom Drama and Theatre, Dance, and Music."

means that we take the long view. Arts are not "efficient"—and what they are effective for, we normally don't measure. The answer to the third question, "How?" depends on answers to the first two questions. That's what this chapter is about.

We have at least five sets of stakeholders: the taxpayers, the students, the educators, businesspeople, and policymakers. It's unlikely that each of them will agree on a common policy and action plan, but we need to address the following issues:

1. Arts are clearly justifiable as an equal and major discipline.

2. The primary benefits of arts are implicit; as secondary and foundational learning, each of which are difficult to assess.

3. Policymakers are driven by the input (money) and output (higher test scores) paradigm of education—the efficiency model.

4. States want to see arts assessed to satisfy themselves that they are using taxpayer money well.

5. What you assess changes how students go about learning. In turn, that will ultimately determine their chances for success.

6. What you assess changes how teachers will feel compelled to go about teaching arts.

7. The measuring of arts may or may not destroy any explicit learning available from them, but it will miss the more subtle but powerful ways which arts enhance seven neurobiological systems. And we may kill off the joy, the love, the sense of wonder and discovery that must go hand in hand with art-making.

Why Arts Should Be Assessed

With increasing attention on test scores, schools want to put on their best face. Arts could be another way to do it. There are several popular reasons for assessing arts:

· Other disciplines are assessed.
· Assessment makes it seem more legitimate.
· They'll get more funding.
· Teachers will pay more attention to it and make sure it happens.
· Testing might make students more accountable for learning arts.
· It will answer the critics who say pro-arts people will waste student time with a "touchy-feely" liberal arts curriculum.

The problem with these arguments is two-fold. First, under scrutiny, none of them hold up. Second, they are all operating out of the old-school paradigm based on a false purpose of education. For example, look at the first item on the list. This common argument is, "After all, everything else is assessed, isn't it?" Not true. Civility is important—every parent, teacher, and district supports it, but it's not measured. Avoiding drug use is important, but how do we assess it? Honesty is important, and so is love of learning. Every parent would tell you they want those qualities or that knowledge, but it's not assessed.

The fact is, many important things are not measured—for a good reason. Just because something is important, that doesn't mean you have to measure it or that there is a sensible way to measure it. But shouldn't arts be held to the same standard as other disciplines? I would argue against that. Other disciplines are learned differently—generally more explicitly. To make disciplines like arts more explicit borders on the ludicrous. "Name five painters from the Impressionist Era." Arts are not that simple. The value of arts is primarily from the internal experiences (our developing mind/body systems and social values) or performance (we are doing art-making). Collecting facts about arts is not doing arts. In real life, arts get reviewed or appreciated, not measured.

How Arts Could Be Assessed

The question I am addressing here is not "Can we?" but "Should we?" Yes, we can assess some obvious elements of arts in the short-term. *But that's not the real value* of arts! Arts should not be taught so a student can identify five 20th century dance steps. This reeks of "cultural literacy." Students will smell out this antiquated 20th century trivia quest and dismiss it. Arts are not for short-term assessment. The current buzzwords are "performance-based assessment" and "higher stakes testing." But that not only misses the point, it's also misleading in terms of what real learning is all about. Perhaps we need to "rethink assessment through the arts," as Dennie Palmer Wolf and Nancy Pistone (1991) have said (see also Bellanca, 1994; Dunn, 1995; Marzano, Pickering, & McTighe, 1993).

The well-intentioned arts advocates who are promoting assessments have engaged their most pragmatic and creative resources to implement a well-rounded system (e.g., Wisconsin Department of

Public Instruction, 1997). Each of the three arts disciplines has its own set of criteria. Several states, ones that have been forward-thinking in their embrace of arts, have produced academic standards for arts. In general, typical arts assessment revolves around three separate strands. Here are some of the real-world ways arts are currently being assessed in this misdirected frenzy of higher stakes testing and educational efficiency. I have taken these from actual arts tests. The names of the assessing agencies have been omitted as a courtesy.

1. Knowledge/Content of That Art

· "Name three wind instruments." (musical, grade 5).

· "Discuss differences in clothing style worn by Native Americans and 16th century African tribesman" (visual arts, grade 3).

· "List the ways that people express themselves with their face and body." (performance arts, grade 3–4).

· "Identify the following artistic styles and describe how you'd decorate a restaurant in these styles: whimsical, analytical, factual, spiritual, and allegorical" (fine arts, grade 8, benchmarks for art structure and function).

· "List the musical instrument types in a symphony orchestra (musical, grade 12).

2. Responses to Art

· "Explain your choices of materials and personal feelings about the decoupage you completed." (visual arts, grade 3–4).

· "Analyze the psychological appeal of advertising in the visual arts." (visual arts, grade 12, benchmarks for art structure and function).

· "Keep a diary about how you felt during the rehearsals for the upcoming play you're in." (performance arts, grade 8).

· "Which instrument is being played during this five-second music clip: Is it a (1) trombone, (2) trumpet, (3) French horn, or (4) tuba?" (Musical arts, grade 5, benchmarks for key competencies).

· "What are some universal themes and structures you hear in music from the Baroque era? (musical arts, grade 8).

· "Compare early Picasso paintings to later Picasso works and discuss the differences." (visual arts, grade 12).

· "Discuss: What role should students play in music censorship?" (musical, grade 5).

3. Performance-Related Questions

• "Create a new soundtrack appropriate for graduation" (performance arts, grade 8).

• "Create a directory of some kind that would be useful to others in the community." (visual arts, grade 12).

• "Demonstrate the differences between skipping, hopping, and leaping." (performance arts, grade 2–3).

• "Create a design blueprint for the best school in the world." (visual arts, grade 5).

• "Learn the main theme of *Haida* by Henry Leck. Sing and record your song in parts and listen to it. Share what the song sounds like to you and what it means to you." (Performing arts, grade 3).

Are these items measurable? Yes, they are. Are any of these tasks worth doing? Some are. In fact, the list presents some interesting and useful questions. Should the arts be quantified to matching standards with other, more knowledge-based disciplines? Only if you are still in the old paradigm of *arts as efficient* (they're not!). Only if you are operating out of the paradigm called, "If it's valuable, we must assess it." (*Who says so?*) And only if you think that schools are in the information business. (*We are in the people business!*). And only if you think that by assessing arts, you'll get better human beings. (*Ask 100 composers, designers, artists, directors, sculptors, musicians, actresses, athletes, engineers, and dancers if early, constant testing would have encouraged them or turned them off in pursuit of an arts career.*) Remember, arts are not efficient, they are not about counting notes, brushstrokes, or dance steps. They are about life, growth, and expanding who we can become as human beings. They are about the long view of life.

Assessment and the Long View

For the longest time, many within the arts community have resisted assessment. Part of their reasoning had to do with a fundamental issue behind arts. Arts, it was been argued, is for cultural, aesthetic, and personal reasons. To that argument, I would add, *"Arts are for the long view."* As an analogy, how do you measure your local ecosystem? You can measure the parts, but the whole? You can take a snapshot, but what about the long-term view? The question of how you measure the ecosystem is not at all trivial. Daily, weekly, and other short-term measures are irrelevant, untimely and probably misleading. What naturalists and ecobiologists have found is that *the only view* of nature is the long view.

Here's an example. A warm winter in the upper Midwest fails to kill off the usual mosquito larvae in a national park. The mosquito population multiplies like crazy, which feeds more fish on the lakes, which feeds more birds. The next winter is a normal cold one; and higher numbers of birds migrate South, creating increased excrement droppings for outdoor-minded tourists 2,000 miles away. The tourists pack up and go to another sunny climate, and the area loses millions in tourist revenues. Local shopkeepers are up in arms and want to shoot the birds. Before you dismiss this as fictional, it has actually happened. The long view says that nature will sort all this out over time, and soon things will be back to usual. It also has something to do with the arts. Arts are not a *strategic* solution (like shooting the birds) to inject into an educational ecosystem to get an immediate result. They are best when implemented over the long haul, with an eye for the future, not the present.

How Traditional Assessment Affects the Arts

Performance-based assessment means that students will be performing arts to get a grade. In physical education, do we grade students on how well they perform in a sport? Or do we grade them on teamwork, enthusiasm, and participation? Over and over, you'll hear this sensible theme: *Engage the learner joyfully, and you'll get results.* Structure, define, and narrow the expression in arts, and you may get students who learn to dislike arts.

Here's the problem I have with these kinds of assessments. Even if students could do all of those items listed earlier (and the rest of the arts being assessed), at each grade level, I have no idea how the arts *really affected them.* Did the arts education they received develop a love for arts in the students? Were they able to express themselves freely? Did the students develop the critical neurobiological systems introduced earlier in this book? Most assessment items won't answer these questions. So if students learn to loathe the arts, if they can't express themselves fully, and if the assessment does not enhance the maturation and development of valuable human qualities and skills, what was the point of it? The answer is, of course, to please the bean-counting poli-cymakers bent on proving that their tax dollar spent in arts is being held accountable. Remember, not everything that's measurable is important, and not everything that's important is measurable.

Difficulty with Arts and Assessment

The development of our art-related biological systems depends on a set of discrete and implicit processes with minimal short-term gain. These systems (perceptual motor, stress, memory, and so forth) make micro-scopic changes that, when applied over months and years, become rel-evant and powerful. These systems, with today's technology, cannot be measured. All measuring of the results of these systems misses the point: *The systems are processes*—the results are too time and context dependent to measure. In six months, keyboard instruction may pro-vide better spatial skills; but in five years, you may get a better listener, stronger math skills, and a more confident and self-disciplined student. Do you have a test for the latter benefits? After all, they're the real ben-efits of the music instruction.

An essential theme of art is creativity, and the assessment of creativi-ty is problematic. Research shows that the focus on grades tends to devaluate learning and creative expression. If you aren't there at the time of art-making, you can't realistically evaluate it. Much of the best art is spontaneous, interactive, or not required. Children, so full of unbridled artistic responses, too often have those responses drummed out of them by middle or high school. By constantly having to prove that their work is worthy, and narrowing their work to gain approval, students lose much of their creativity. Doing color by the numbers is not art. In other words, you can get students to do art, but the product you'll get will be different. The student mentality becomes, "Tell me what I need to do to get a good grade, and I'll do that."

The grade, not learning or mastery, becomes the goal. We risk driv-ing away the love of learning; and the kids who need it the most will have one more hurdle to overcome. Kids will learn the game fast and play the game instead of doing arts because it moves them. If high arts scores become important, the arts will, like other disciplines, become a victim of student cheating and enormous teacher subjectivity.

Arts programs are not efficient and should not try to focus on effi-ciency. Arts induce change in the brain slowly, in stages and in ways we're not yet prepared to measure. Character building is inefficient, mastery in learning is inefficient, friendships are inefficient, and arts are inefficient. The things we value the most are inefficient. They all develop slowly and over time.

Arts provide learners with the opportunity to develop specialized brain systems, none of which are easy to quantify because they are the *processes* that allow for *later* results (see Figure 5.1). Because these processes are not the results, testing the processes instead of results may encourage students to narrow their artistic input in hopes of a focusing on a better grade.

FIGURE 5.1
ART-MAKING DEVELOPS MOST OF OUR ESSENTIAL NEUROBIOLOGICAL SYSTEMS

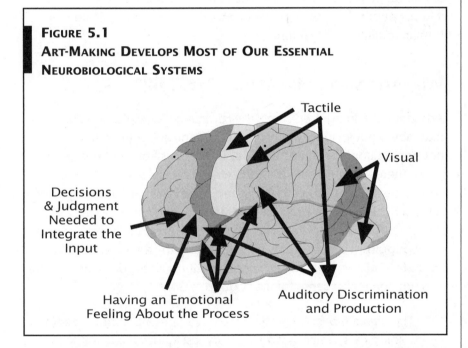

Many educators—and parents—argue that the focus on test scores instead of learning alters the student experience dramatically and often brings out the worst in students. In state after state, cheating on the standardized state exams is becoming more common. Some teachers are sharing answers with kids, teaching to the test, and trading test information with other teachers. Now far too many teachers spend more of their time teaching to the test instead of teaching to the real interests of the students. Some districts require that all teachers' scores be posted, adding to the threat and intimidation factor. This is not helpful in any area, but it is particularly devastating in the arts.

> **M**ost of what we can measure now, behaviorally, is neurologically immaterial to the optimal development of the brain.

Arts—musical, visual, and dramatic arts, as well as physical education—may be to learning what parental love is to a child: Often invisible, impossible to measure, but it's what makes all the difference. We have an ethical and moral responsibility—some might argue, a mandate—to the learners of tomorrow to support arts programs.

The fundamental question facing education today is simple: "Is our social, moral, and ethical mandate to maximize test scores or to prepare the citizens for tomorrow? Are students (and their test scores) to be used as a marketing tool for ambitious politicians? Are our schools, whether charter, voucher, private, or public, fair game for the economic and moral equivalent of Russian roulette with our future?

Why Arts Should Be Made "Pass/Fail"

Arts should be integrated across the curriculum. Can you think of a class that should not include music, graphic organizers, or movement? I cannot. Some people are currently assessing the arts—but in traditional ways. There are plenty of insightful, well-disciplined academics and other assessment consultants who can and have created thorough arts rubrics. But I advocate a middle ground between matching the assessment methods of the other major disciplines and virtually no accountability (Stiggins, 1993; Wiggins, 1993). Making the arts courses "pass/fail," allows for an emphasis on continuous feedback, not grades. This position makes sense for many good reasons:

· The ultimate passing grade is the development of the student's neurobiological systems, not an arbitrary test in the arts.
· It allows students to pursue the arts for the sheer joy of it.
· It gives students more responsibility for their own progress.
· The grading process becomes time consuming. Valuable time is spent on assessing that could have been spent on art-making.
· Students become more interested in mastery and less interested in just trying to get by.
· An integrated arts curriculum will encourage students to want to take the classes that focus on their individual favorite areas of art.
· It allows arts to become cultural and to encourage diversity without becoming pedantic.

· A simple process-portfolio can store artifacts, journals, and work samples without the hassle of grading.

· Teachers and students can work collaboratively to reach a common goal instead of being adversarial.

· Students can explore their creative interests without trying to please a teacher or narrowing their focus to grade-related outcomes.

How to Implement Pass/Fail Arts Standards

In this system, students are guided by the teacher, who explains the learning outcomes, provides tools for success, and helps make them relevant. Students focus more on doing the "right work" than on "doing the work right." To get a "pass" grade, students must meet the following requirements:

1. Have Good Attendance. There's a standard set by the teacher or the arts curriculum designers that must be met to ensure that the most essential art-making neurobiological processes get the time needed to develop. It might be a minimum of 80 percent or more.

2. Participate in Activities. This means that students may not opt out of an activity they don't like. It means that although there may be choice in the types of art-making available, one choice *not* available is inactivity.

3. Develop an Agreed-on Portfolio of Work. A simple "Processfolio" is kept by the student. This might consist of a huge envelope or box that is filled with artifacts, journals, work samples, learning logs, interviews, peer feedback, tape recordings, art videos, and a learning profile. This creates a better, more accountable link between what work activities are required and what's being produced. Teachers should allow time for students to browse their portfolio, reflect on progress, and reset goals.

4. Get Frequent Feedback on Their Processfolio. There's no way a teacher could possibly provide enough feedback on each student's art progress. Instead, the teachers uses several ways to ensure that students get feedback on their work. These would include peer editing, peer rubrics, learning logs, matching work with agreed-on activity checklists, gallery walks, questionnaires, peer observation, feedback by adults outside of class, video observation, and trial and error results.

5. Participate in Student/Teacher Conferences. In addition to all the other less formalized forms of feedback, teachers should meet for a few minutes with every student informally, to walk through their processfolio and ensure that it matches up with the other pass/fail criteria. More important, it allows time for visiting, debriefing, and reflection—what worked, what didn't, and what could work better. These conferences help form the basis for the final determination of either "pass" or "fail."

Arts Make a Difference

Arts can enhance the neurobiological systems mentioned in this book. They include our cognitive, emotional, attentional, and immune systems. Art-making helps students acquire a feel for what it means to transform an idea into a product or art form. Art-making will refine, in the learners, a heightened awareness of the senses. Students will gain aesthetic qualities of art from building a cabinet, playing an instrument, making an instrument, or completing a dance step. They will be able to apply these qualities to life, but that's not the only point of it.

Students will be creating new ideas and will likely develop a willingness to imagine and explore ideas that have not existed before. Art-making students will be willing to explore uncertainty, delaying closure or early solutions in favor of sustaining judgment and enhanced process. Students will learn alternative thinking. They'll be more willing to explore opposing ideas, multiple perspectives, and unexpected points of view. They'll become more compassionate about others' feelings. They'll appreciate better other cultures and alternative ways of thinking. If you like those qualities, arts can help instill them better than any other discipline.

The beauty of arts is that they are both deep and wide in their benefits. They can improve nearly everything that schools need today: self-esteem, health, inclusion, motivation, attendance, grades, community involvement, and communication skills, as the landmark report *Champions of Change* has pointed out (Catterall et al., 1999; Fiske, 1999). The arts bring these benefits because they work on multiple biological systems. Remember, arts programs have to be well designed, integrated, and fully supported. But when they're done well, nothing else comes as close in delivering "bang for the buck."

Summary and Policy Implications

Arts are beneficial and are clearly justifiable as an equal and major discipline. It is also clear that the quantity and quality of short-term, immediate arts benefits are minimal compared to the long-term benefits. The biggest issue is one of educating policymakers who are driven by the old factory-model school paradigms. Read the following list closely—these qualities are all straight from the 20th century factory model. These out-dated paradigms are based on the following:

1. Efficiency: The ratio of input (money) to output (higher test scores). In this model, less money spent to get higher scores is clearly valued. But what about the money spent for things that lead to better people, not test scores?

2. Appearances: This is called "looking good." Policymakers want to see arts assessed to satisfy themselves that they are using taxpayer money well. If students don't do well, at least they were accountable through testing.

3. Business Model: Many people are more comfortable with the model of regurgitation. Schools give information to students; they prove they know it on a test.

Let's reconsider each of those old-style paradigms in light of what we now know:

· The *efficiency model* works only on factories, in businesses, and on machines. It *does not work* when it comes to developing complex neurobiological systems involving aesthetics, a subject matter bias, perceptual motor skills, cultural awareness, or spatial reasoning.

· *Appearance* is a significant issue. Policymakers who advocate and implement arts are afraid that they won't have a paper trail to justify making them mandatory. But *you can have* a good paper trail, based on a well-documented pass-fail system. It is evident through the use of processfolios. Once this becomes obvious, attitudes will change.

· The *business model of schools* is changing; it's just slow. The old paradigm was that schools had teachers who knew a lot, so if you paid attention, you could learn from them. But today's students can get information (more of it, newer, and in more depth) from other sources. The message here is that schools will become increasingly irrelevant if they function solely as an information giver and tester. But schools should be about people, not data. Schools provide powerful social contexts for orchestrated, meaningful experiences. If schools forget that, they'll become dinosaurs; and the online, downloadable grade K–12 school concept will destroy public schools in our lifetime. If we are in the people business, arts ought to play a major part of the learning experience.

■ ■ ■

The so-called "new models" have long been in place in some public and many private schools. I opened this book describing a Waldorf school, and there are countless other schools that beautifully integrate arts without any letter-grade assessment. What you assess changes how students go about learning. *What* you assess changes *how* teachers will feel about teaching the arts. The measuring of arts may not destroy the learning available from them, but it will miss the complex, subtle, but powerful ways in which arts enhance our lives. We may kill off the joy, the love, the sense of wonder and discovery that must go hand in hand with learning. Arts are the "goose." Let's not kill the goose that lays the golden eggs.

Appendix: Additional Resources

Useful Web Sites

American Choral Directors Association:
    http://www.choralnet.org/acda/index.htm

American Music Conference: http://www.amc-music.com

American Music Therapy Association: http://www.musictherapy.org

ArtsEdge: http://artsedge.kennedy-center.org/ir/music.html

Arts Education Partnership on the World Wide Web: http://aep-arts.org/

ArtsUSA for the American Council for the Arts: http://www.artsusa.org

Association for the Advancement of Arts Education: http://www.aaae.org/

Educational Kinesiology Foundation: http://www.braingym.org/

International Association of Jazz Educators:
    http://www.jazzcentralstation.com/iaje

International Society for Music Education (ISME): http://www.isme.org

MuSICA—Music & Science Information Computer Archive:
    http://www.musica.uci.edu

Music Education Research Base: http://www.ffa.ucalgary.ca/merb/

Music Education Search System: http://www.music.utah.edu/MESS/

Music Educators National Conference (MENC): http://www.menc.org

National Art Education Association (NAEA): http://www.naea-reston.org

National Association of Teachers of Singing: http://www.nats.org

National Dance Association: http://www.aahperd.org/nda/nda.html

National Music Council: http://www.musiccouncil.org/

Organization of American Kodaly Educators (OAKE): http://oake.org

Research Journal of the Florida Music Educators Association:
    http://arts.usf.edu/music/rpme.html

Research Journals in Music Education: http://www.ed.uiuc.edu/EdPsy-387/Tina-Scott/project/major-journals.html

Texas Cultural and Arts Network (TCAnet): http://www.arts.state.tx.us/school_house/music.htm

Music-Related Training Organizations

Institute of Music, Health & Education (Mozart Effect), Boulder, Colorado: Telephone: (800) 721-2177

Tomatis Sound Listening & Learning Center, Phoenix, Arizona: Telephone: (602) 381-0086

Suzuki Association, Boulder, Colorado: Telephone: (303) 444-0948

Brain-Based Learning Materials

For brain-based educator and trainer products (including videos, books, downloadable books, special brain reports, CDs, brain models, etc.):

ASCD's Online Store: http://www.ascd.org · toll-free (800) 933-2723 · fax (703) 575-5400

The Brain Store: http://www.thebrainstore.com · toll-free (800) 325-4769 · fax (858) 546-7560

3-Day Brain/Mind Learning Expo

Twice a year, there's a comprehensive, practical 3-Day Brain/Mind Expo. You can hear author Eric Jensen and over 50 other first-class speakers. It's a way to stay up-to-date, network with others, and learn how to apply cutting-edge brain-based learning to every discipline, including arts. More information at http://www.brainexpo.com or call (858) 546-7555.

References and Bibliography

Alexander, M., & Beatty, L. (1996, May). Music improves emotional awareness (letter). *Family Medicine, 28*(5), 318.

Allen, L. S., & Gorski, R. A. (1991). Sexual dimorphism of the anterior commissure and massa intermedia of the human brain. *Journal of Comparative Neurology, 312,* 97–104.

Allman, J. M. (1999). *Evolving brains.* New York: Scientific American Library.

Amabile, T. (1986). Social influences on creativity: The effects of contracted-for reward. *Journal of Personality and Social Psychology, 50*(1), 14–23.

Armstrong, C. L. (1994). *Designing assessment in art.* Reston, VA: National Art Education Association.

Barker, R., & Barasi, S. (1999). *Neuroscience at a glance* (pp. 60–61). Oxford, London: Blackwell Science Ltd.

Barnet, A. (2000, June). There's joy in Harlem. *Reader's Digest,* pp. 130–136.

Bazzano, C., Cunningham, L. N., Varrassi, G., & Falconio, T. (1992). Health related fitness and blood pressure in boys and girls ages 10–17 years. *Pediatric Exercise Science, 4,* 128–135.

Bellanca, J. (1994). *Multiple assessments for multiple intelligences.* Palatine, IL: IRI/Skylight.

Benson, N. J., Lovett, M. W., & Kroeber, C. L. (1997). Training and transfer of learning effects in disabled and normal readers: Evidence of specific deficits. *Journal of Experimental Child Psychology, 64,* 343–366.

Benton, W. (Ed.). (1986). Montessori system. In *The new encyclopedia Britannica* (Vol. 17, p. 787). Chicago: Encyclopedia Brittanica.

Berry, L. H. (1991). *Visual complexity and pictorial memory: A fifteen year research perspective.* Paper presented at the annual meeting of the Association for Educational Communications and Technology. (ERIC Document Reproduction Service No. ED 334 974)

Berthoz, A. (2000). *The brain's sense of movement.* Cambridge, MA: Harvard University Press.

Beyers, J. (1998, June). The biology of human play. *Child Development, 69*(3), 599–600.

Bezruczko, N., & Schroeder, D. H. (1996, May). The development of visual preferences in art-trained and non-art-trained schoolchildren. *Genetic, Social, and General Psychology Monographs, 122*(2), 179–196.

Biddle, S., & Armstrong, N. (1992). Children's physical activity: An exploratory study of psychological correlates. *Social Science Medicine, 34*(3), 325–331.

Bjorkland, D. F., & Brown, R. D. (1998). Physical play and cognitive development: Integrating activity, cognition, and education. *Child Development, 69*(3), 604–606.

Blood, D. J., & Ferriss, S. J. (1993, February). Effects of background music on anxiety, satisfaction with communication, and productivity. *Psychological Reports, 72*(1), 171–177.

Boone, R. T., & Cunningham, J. G. (1998, September). Children's decoding of emotion in expressive body movement: The development of cue attunement. *Developmental Psychology, 34*(5), 1007–1016.

Brownley, K. A., McMurray, R. G., & Hackney, A. C. (1995). Effects of music on physiological and affective responses to graded treadmill exercise in trained and untrained runners. *International Journal of Psychophysiology, 19*(3), 193–201.

Bryan, T., Sullivan-Burstein, K., & Mathur, S. (1998). The influence of affect on social information processing. *Journal of Learning Disabilities, 31*, 418–426.

Burton, J., Horowitz, R., & Abeles, H. (1999). Learning in and through the arts: Curriculum implications. In E. Fiske (Ed.), *Champions of change: The impact of the arts on learning.* [Online report]. Washington, DC: The Arts Education Partnership and the President's Committee on the Arts and the Humanities. Available: http://www.artsedge.kennedy-center.org/champions/

Burz, H., & Marshall, K. (1999). *Performance-based curriculum for music and the visual arts.* Thousand Oaks, CA: Corwin Press.

Byers, J. A. (1998, June). The biology of human play. *Child Development, 69*(3), 599–600.

Byers, J. A., & Walker, C. (1995). Refining the motor training hypothesis for the evolution of play. *American Naturalist, 146*, 25–40.

Cahill, L., Prins, B., Weber, M., & McGaugh, J. (1994, October 20). Adrenergic activation and memory for emotional events. *Nature, 371*(6499), 702–704.

Calfas, K. J., & Taylor, W. C. (1994). Effects of physical activity on psychological variables in adolescents. *Pediatric Exercise Science, 6*(4), 406–423

Calvin, W. (1996). *How brains think.* New York: Basic Books.

Cameron, J. (1992). *The artist's way: A spiritual path to higher creativity.* New York: J. P. Tarcher/Putnam Books

Campbell, D. (1997). *The Mozart effect.* New York: Avon Books.

Campeau, R. (1990) *Changing the level of aesthetic, verbal and visual responses of rural high school students in a one year studio art course.* New York: National Arts Education Research Center, New York University.

Carmichael, K., & Atchinson, D. (1997). Music and play therapy: Playing my feelings. *International Journal of Play Therapy, 6*, 63–72.

Caterino, M. C., & Polak, E. D. (1999, August). Effects of two types of activity on the performance of 2nd, 3rd and 4th grade students on a test of concentration. *Perceptual & Motor Skills, 89*(1), 245–248.

Catterall, J. S., Chapleau, R., & Iwanaga, J. (1999). Involvement in the arts and human development: General involvement and intensive involvement in music and theater arts. In E. Fiske (Ed.), *Champions of change: The impact of the arts on learning.* [Online report]. Washington, DC: The Arts Education Partnership and the President's Committee on the Arts and the Humanities. Available: http://www.artsedge.kennedy-center.org/champions/

Chan, A. S., Ho, Y. C., & Cheung, M. C. (1998). Music training improves verbal memory. *Nature, 396*(607), 128.

Charnetski, C., & Brennan Jr., F. (1998). Effect of music and auditory stimuli on secretory immunoglobulin A (IgA). *Perceptual and Motor Skills, 87,* 1163–1170.

Chase, M. (1993, October 31). Inner music: Imagination may play a role in how the brain learns muscle control. *Wall Street Journal, 124,* A1.

Clark, A. (1997). *Being there.* Cambridge, MA: MIT Press.

Cockerton, T., Moore, S., & Norman, D. (1997). Cognitive test performance and background music. *Perceptual and Motor Skills, 85,* 1435–1438.

Coe, K. (1990). *Art, the replicable unit: Identifying the origin of art in human prehistory.* Paper presented at the annual meeting of Human Behavior and Evolution Society, Los Angeles.

Cohen, E. P., & Gainer, R. S. (1995). *Art: Another language for learning* (3rd ed.). Portsmouth, NH: Heinemann. (ERIC Document Reproduction Service No. 383 640)

College Board, Office of Academic Affairs. (1983). *Academic preparation for college.* New York: Author.

College Board. (2000). *The College Board: Preparing, inspiring, and connecting.* [Online]. Available: http://www.collegeboard.org/prof/

Colwell, C. M. (1994). Therapeutic application of music in the whole language kindergarten. *Journal of Music Therapy, 31,* 238–247.

Cooper, K. J. (1999, November 26). Study says natural classroom lighting can aid achievement. *The Washington Post,* A14.

Corso, M. (1997, April 9). *Children who desperately want to read, but are not working at grade level: Use movement patterns as "windows" to discover why.* Paper presented at the annual international conference of the Association for Children's Education, Portland, OR. (ERIC Document Reproduction Service No. CS 012 660)

Cranz, G. (1998). *The chair: Rethinking culture, body and design* (pp. 60–63, 95–135, 181–197). New York: W. W. Norton.

Cushman, W. H., & Brian, C. (1987). Illumination. In G. Salvendy (Ed.), *Handbook of human factors* (pp. 671–680). New York: Wiley.

Darby, J., & Catterall, J. (1994, Winter). The fourth R: The arts and learning. *Teachers College Record, 96*(2), 299–328.

Davidson, J. (1996). My block and beyond: A documentation of how drawing in conjunction with writing contributes to the thinking process. In *The Arts.* Albany: New York State Education Department. (ERIC Document Reproduction Service No. ED 406 300)

Davis, J. (1997). *Mapping the mind: The secrets of the human brain and how it works.* Secaucus, NJ: Carol Publishing Group.

Dehaene, S., Spelke, E., Pinel, P., Stanescu, R., & Tvisikin, S. (1999, May 7). Sources of mathematical thinking: Behavioral and brain-imaging evidence. *Science, 284,* 970–974.

Demany, L., McKenzie, B., & Vurpillot, E. (1970). Rhythm perception in early infancy. *Nature, 226*(5604), 718–719.

Dennison, P., & Dennison, G. (1989). *Brain gym, teacher's edition.* Ventura, CA: Edu-Kinesthetics. Information available: http://www.braingym.org/

Dewey, J. (1934). *Art as experience.* New York: Minion Ballet Publishers.

Diamond, M., & Hopson, J. (1998). *Magic trees of the mind.* New York: Penguin Group.

Dissanayake, E. (1988). *What is art for?* Seattle: University of Washington Press.

Dissanayake, E. (1992). *Homo aestheticus: Where art comes from and why.* Seattle: University of Washington Press.

Douglas, S., & Willatts, P. (1994). Musical ability enhances reading skills. *Journal of Research in Reading, 17,* 99–107.

Dunn, P. (1995). *Creating curriculum in art.* Reston, VA: National Art Education Association.

Dwyer, T., Blizzard, L., & Dean, K. (1996, April). Physical activity and performance in children. *Nutrition Reviews, 54*(4), 27–32.

Eastman, M., & Kamon, E. (1976, February). Posture and subjective evaluation at flat and slanted desks. *Human Factors, 18*(1), 15–26.

Edgerton, C. L. (1994). The effect of improvisational music therapy on the communicative behaviors of autistic children. *Journal of Music Therapy, 1,* 31–62.

Eisner, E. (1998, September–October). Does experience in the arts boost academic achievement? *Arts Education, 51*(1), 5–15.

Elbert, T., Pantev, C., Weinbruch, C., Rockstroh, B., & Taub, E. (1995). Increased auditory cortical representation of the left hand in string players. *Science, 270,* 305–307.

Ericksson, P. S., Perfilieva, E., Bjork-Eriksson, T., Alborn, A. M., Nordborg, C., Peterson, D. A., & Gage, F. (1998, November). Neurogenesis in the adult human hippocampus. *Nature Medicine, 4*(11), 1313–1317.

Escher, J., & Evequoz, D. (1999, May 20). Music and heart rate variability. Study of the effect of music on heart rate variability in healthy adolescents. *Schweizerische Rundschau für Medizin Praxis, 88*(21), 951–952.

Farrell, M. (1973, Spring). Music and self-esteem: Disadvantaged problem boys in an all-black elementary school. *Journal of Research in Music Education, 21*(1), 80–84.

Fehrs-Rampolla, B. (1990). *Affecting students' critical thinking and aesthetic attitudes utilizing the ceramic arts of non-Western culture.* New York: National Arts Education Research Center, New York University.

Fiske, E. (Ed.). (1999). *Champions of change: The impact of the arts on learning.* [Online report]. Washington, DC: The Arts Education Partnership and the President's Committee on the Arts and the Humanities. Available: http://www.artsedge.kennedy-center.org/champions/

Flynn, J. E. (1987). Interim study of procedures for investigating the effect of light on impression and behavior. *Journal of Illuminating Engineering Society, 3,* 87–94.

Forster, J., & Strack, F. (1998). Subjective theories about encoding may influence judgmental regulation in human memory. *Social Cognition, 16,* 78–92.

Frith, U., & Happe, F. (1994). Autism: Beyond "theory of mind." *Cognition, 50,* 115–132.

Funk, A. (1992, November 8). Art integral part of learning. *The Topeka Capital-Journal,* p. 2C.

Gao, J. H., Parsons, L. M., Bower, J. M., Xiong, J., Li, J., & Fox, P. T. (1996, April 26). Cerebellum implicated in sensory acquisition and discrimination rather than motor control. *Science, 272*(5261), 482–483.

Gardiner, M. (1996). Learning improved by arts training. Scientific Correspondence in *Nature, 381*(580), 284.

Gardner, H. (1983). *Frames of mind* (pp. 99–127). New York: Basic Books.

Gardner, H. (1999). *The disciplined mind* (p. 82). New York: Simon & Schuster.

Gardstrom, S. C. (1999). Music exposure and criminal behavior: Perceptions of juvenile offenders. *Journal of Music Therapy, 36*(3), 207–221.

Garreau, B. (1994). Evidence of abnormal processing of auditory stimulation observed in cerebral blood flow studies. *Developmental Brain Dysfunction, 7,* 119–128.

Gerber, S. (1996). Extracurricular activities and academic achievement. *Journal of Research and Development in Education, 30*(1), 42–50.

Gibbons, D., Ebbeck, V., & Weiss, M. (1995, September). Fair play for kids: Effects on the moral development of children in physical education. *Quarterly for Exercise and Sport, 66*(3), 247.

Gilbert, A. G. (1977). *Teaching the 3 R's through movement experiences.* New York: Macmillan.

Gilmore, T. M. (1982). *Results of a survey of children's performance on a variety of psychological tests before and after completing the Tomatis program.* Rexale, Ontario, Canada: MDS Health Group Ltd.

Godeli, M. R., Santana, P. R., Souza, V. H., & Marquetti, G. P. (1996). Influence of background music on preschooler's behavior: A naturalistic approach. *Perceptual and Motor Skills, 82,* 1123–1129.

Goleman, D. (1995). *Emotional intelligence* (p. 34). New York: Bantam Books.

Gomez-Pinilla, F., So, V., & Kesslak, J. P. (1998, July). Spatial learning and physical activity contribute to the induction of fibroblast growth factor: Neural substrates for increased cognition associated with exercise. *Neuroscience, 85*(1), 53–61.

Gomez-Shafer, G. (1990). *Evaluating Mexican and Mexican American students' perception of the work of Mexican artists versus Western artists.* New York: National Arts Education Research Center, New York University.

Graziano, A., Peterson, M., & Shaw, G. (1999, March). Enhanced learning of proportional math through music training and spatial-temporal training. *Neurological Research, 21*(2), 139–152.

Greenfield, P. M., & Schneider, L. (1977). Building a tree structure: The development of hierarchical complexity and interrupted strategies in children's construction activity. *Developmental Psychology, 3,* 299–313.

Gregorian, V. (1997, March 23). Ten things you can do to make our schools better. *Parade Magazine,* 6–7.

Gresh, R. (1990). *Heightening aesthetic response through the development and production of student-created videos.* New York: National Arts Education Research Center, New York University.

Grieco, A. (1986). Sitting posture: An old problem and a new one. *Ergonomics, 29*(3), 345–362.

Grimsrud, T. (1990). Humans were not created to sit—and why you have to refurnish your life. *Ergonomics, 33*(3), 291.

Griss, S. (1994, February). Creative movement: A language for learning. *Educational Leadership, 51*(5). [Online article]. Available: http:/www.ascd.org/frameedlead.html

Griss, S. (1998). *Minds in motion*. Portsmouth, NH: Heinemann.

Guiard, Y. (1987). Asymmetric division of labor in human skilled bimanual action: The kinetic chain as model. *Journal of Motor Behavior, 19*(4), 486–517.

Gunsberg, A. (1991). Play as improvisation: The benefits of music for developmentally delayed young children's social play. *Early Child Development and Care, 66,* 85–91.

Habermeyer, S. (1999). *Good music, brighter children*. Rocklin CA: Prima Publishing.

Hall, J. (1952, February). The effect of background music on the reading comprehension of 278 eighth and ninth graders. *Journal of Educational Research, 45,* 451–458.

Hallet, M. (1999, May). *Gray matters: Sports, fitness and the brain*. Transcript from National Public Radio (NPR). Dr. Mark Hallet was interviewed by Frank Gifford. Available from NPR at 800-652-7246.

Hamann, D., Bourassa, R. & Aderman, M. (1991). Arts experiences and creativity scores of high school students. *Contributions of Music Education, 14,* 36–37.

Hannaford, C. (1995). *Smart moves*. Arlington, VA: Great Ocean Publishing.

Harth, E. (1999, June/July). The emergence of art and language in the human brain. Art and the brain. *Journal of Consciousness Studies, 6*(6–7), 97–115.

Healy, J. (1994). *Your child's growing brain*. New York: Doubleday Books.

Heschong Mahone Consulting Group. (1999). *Daylighting and productivity: Daylighting and schools*. [Online Executive Summary]. Sacramento, CA: Author. Available: http://h-m-g.com/

Hodges, D. (1996). *Handbook of music psychology*. San Antonio: IMR Press.

Hoffman, D. (1998). *Visual intelligence: How we create what we see* (pp. 13–29, 175–181). New York: Norton.

Hoskins, C. (1988). Use of music to increase verbal response and improve expressive language abilities of preschool language delayed children. *Journal of Music Therapy, 25,* 73–84.

Hubel, D. H., & Wiesel, T. N. (1970). The period of susceptibility to the physiological effects of unilateral eye closure in kittens. *Journal of Physiology, 206,* 419–436.

Hume, K. M., & Crossman, J. (1992). Musical reinforcement of practice behaviors among competitive swimmers. *Journal of Applied Behavior Analysis, 25*(2), 665–670.

Hurwitz, I., Wolff, P. H., Bortnick, B. D., & Kokas, K. (1975). Nonmusical effects of the Kodaly music curriculum in primary grade children. *Journal of Learning Disabilities, 8,* 45–51.

Hyerle, D. (1996). *Visual tools for constructing knowledge*. Alexandria, VA: Association for Supervision and Curriculum Development.

Jarnow, J (1991). *All ears: How to use and choose recorded music for children*. New York: Viking.

Jeannerod, M. (1997). *The cognitive neuroscience of action* (p. 289). Cambridge, MA: Blackwell.

Jensen, R. (1999). *The dream society: How the coming shift from information to imagination will transform your business.* New York: McGraw-Hill.

Jing, J., Yuan, C., & Liu, J. (1999, May). Study of human figure drawings in learning disabilities. *Chinese Mental Health Journal, 13*(3), 133–134.

Johnson, J., Petsche, H., Richter, P., von Stein, A., & Filz, O. (1996). The dependence of coherence estimates of spontaneous EEG on gender and music training. *Music Perception, 13,* 563–582.

Johnston, V. (1999). *Why we feel the way we feel* (pp. 73–82). Cambridge, MA: Perseus Books.

Jourdain, R. (1997). *Music, ecstasy and the brain* (pp. 114–137). New York: William Morrow and Co.

Kalmar, M. (1982). The effects of music education based on Kodaly's directives in nursery school children—From a psychologist's point of view. [Special Issue.] *Psychology of Music,* 63–68.

Kantrowitz, B., & Leslie, C. (1997, April 14). Readin', writin', rhythm. *Newsweek,* 71.

Kay, S., & Subotnik, R. (1994). Talent beyond words: Unveiling spatial, expressive, kinesthetic and musical talent in young children. *Gifted Child Quarterly, 38,* 70–74.

Kearney, P. (1996, August 3). Brain research shows importance of arts in education. *The Minneapolis Star Tribune,* p. 19A.

Klinke, R., Kral, A., Heid, S., Tillein, J., & Hartmann, R. (1999, September 10). Recruitment of the auditory cortex in congenitally deaf cats by long-term cochlear electrostimulation. *Science, 285*(5434), 1729–1733.

Konishi, M.. (1994). Pattern generation in birdsong. *Current Opinions in Neurobiology, 4,* 827–831.

Kosslyn, S. (1996). *Image and brain* (pp. 122–124). Cambridge, MA: Bradford Books, MIT Press.

Kratus, J. (1989). A time analysis of the compositional processes used by children ages 7 to 11. *Journal of Research in Music Education, 37,* 5–20.

Kratus, J. (1994). Relationships among children's audiation and their compositional processes and products. *Journal of Research in Music Education, 42,* 115–130.

Krumhans, C. L., & Jusczyk, P. W. (1990). Infants' perception of phrase structure in music. *Psychological Science, 1,* 70–73.

Kyle, N. (1990). *Developing a high school art curriculum to increase aesthetic awareness through the study of process of perception and analysis using three-dimensional art forms.* New York: National Arts Education Research Center, New York University.

Lamb, S. J., & Gregory, A. H. (1993). The relationship between music and reading in beginning readers. *Educational Psychology, 13,* 19–26.

Lane, D. (1992). The effect of a single music therapy session on hospitalized children as measured by salivary immunoglobulin A. (Measuring speech pause time and using Patient Opinion Likert Scale). *Dissertation Abstracts International, 52*(7-B), 3522.

Leroux, C., & Grossman, R. (1999, October 21). Arts in the schools paint master-piece: Higher scores. *Chicago Tribune,* p. A-1.

Longo, P. (1999, November 8). *Distributed knowledge in the brain: Using visual thinking networking to improve student learning.* From a talk given at the Learning and Brain Conference, Boston.

Malyarenko, T. N., Kuraev, G. A., Malyarenko, Y. E., Khvatova, M. V., Romanova, N. G., & Gurina, V. I. (1996). The development of brain's electric activity in 4-yr.-old children by long-term sensory stimulation with music. *Human Physiology, 23,* 76–81.

Mandal, A. (1982, June). The correct height of school furniture. *Human Factors, 24*(3), 257–269.

Mann, L. (1999, August). Dance education: The ultimate sport. *Education Update, 41*(5), 3.

Marantz, K. (1998, November). Learning in and through art: A guide to discipline-based art education. *School Arts, 98*(3), 50.

Martens, F. (1982). Daily physical education. *Journal of Physical Education, Recreation and Dance, 53*(3), 55–58.

Marzano, R. J., Pickering, D., & McTighe, J. (1993). *Assessing student outcomes: Performance assessment using the Dimensions of Learning model.* Alexandria, VA: Association for Supervision and Curriculum Development.

McClelland, J. L., McNaughton, B. L., & O'Reilly, R. C. (1995). Why are there complementary learning systems in the hippocampus and neocortex: Insights from the success and failures of connectionist models of learning and memory. *Psychological Review, 102,* 419–457.

McCraty, R., Atkinson, M., Rein, G., & Watkins, A. D. (1996). Music enhances the effect of positive emotional state on salivary IgA. *Stress Medicine, 12,* 67–75.

McCune, L. (1998, June). The immediate and ultimate functions of physical activity play. *Child Development, 69*(3), 601–603.

McIntosh, R. (1995, December). *School Arts, 95*(4), 33.

McKinnery, C., & Tims, F. (1995). Differential effects of selected classical music on the imagery of high versus low imagers: Two studies. *Journal of Music Therapy, 22*(1), 22–45.

McNeal, R. (1995, January). Extracurricular activities and high school dropouts. *Sociology of Education, 68,* 62–81.

Michaud, E., & Wild, R. (1991). *Boost your brain power.* Emmaus, PA: Rodale Press.

Michon, J. A. (1977). Holes in the fabric of subjective time. *Acta Psychologica, 41,* 191–203.

Miluk-Kolasa, B., Obminski, S., Stupnicki, R., & Golec, L. (1994). Effects of music treatment on salivary cortisol in patients exposed to pre-surgical stress. *Experimental and Clinical Endocrinology, 102*(2), 118–20.

Mockel, M., Rocker, L., Stork, T., Vollert, J., Danne, O., Eichstadt, H., Muller, R., & Hochrein, H. (1994). Immediate physiological responses of healthy volunteers to different types of music: Cardiovascular, hormonal and mental changes. *European Journal of Applied Physiology, 68,* 451–459.

Mohanty, B., & Hejmandi, A. (1992). Effects of intervention training on some cognitive abilities of preschool children. *Psychological Studies, 37,* 31–37.

Monaghan, P. (1998). Does practice shape the brain? *Nature, 394,* 434.

Mooney, R. L., & Smilansky, S. (1973). *An experiment in the use of drawing to promote cognitive development in disadvantaged preschool children in*

Israel and the United States: Final report. Columbus: Ohio State University, Research Foundation. (ERIC Document Reproduction Service No. ED 082842)

Morton, L. L., Pietrangelo, M. C., & Belleperche, S. (1998, Summer). Using music to enhance competence. *Canadian Music Educator, 39*(4), 13–16.

Mosseri, R. (1998). Changing the culture of violence: A seven day admission to a secure unit provides a powerful norm in residential care. *Residential Treatment for Children & Youth, 16*(1), 1–9.

Music Educators National Conference. (2000). S*AT scores of students in the arts.* [Online]. Reston, VA: Author. Available: http://www.menc.org/information/advocate/sat.html

National Center for Education Statistics (NCES). (1998). *Mini-digest of education statistics* (pp. 34–35). Washington, DC: NCES, U.S. Department of Education.

Newcomer, J. W., Selke, G., Melson, A. K., Hershey, T., Craft, S., Richards, K., & Alderson, A. L. (1999, June). Decreased memory performance in healthy humans induced by stress-level cortisol treatment. *Archives of General Psychiatry, 56*(6), 527–533.

Noettcher, W., Hahn, S., & Shaw, G. (1994). Mathematics and music: A search for insight into higher brain function. *Leonardo Music Journal, 4,* 53–58.

Olsho, L. W. (1984). Infant frequency discrimination. *Infant Behavior and Development, 7,* 27–35.

Oppenheimer, T. (1999, September). Schooling the imagination. *Atlantic Monthly, 284*(3), 71–83.

Organization of American Kodaly Educators (OAKE). (2000). *Information about OAKE.* [Online]. Available: http://oake.org/directory/oake_info.html

Ott, J. N. (1985). Color and light: Their effects on plants, animals and people. *Journal of Biosocial Research, 7,* part 1.

Palmer, C. (1997). Music performance. *Annual Review of Psychology, 48,* 115–138.

Palmer, L. (1980, September). Auditory discrimination development through vestibulo-cochlear stimulation. *Academic Therapy, 16*(1), 55–68.

Pantev, C., Oostenveld, R., Engelien, A., Ross, B., Roberts, L., & Hoke, M. (1998). Increased cortical representation in musicians. Scientific Correspondence in *Nature, 396*(128), 811–813.

Parsons, L. M., Martinez, M. J., Delosh, E. D., Halpern, A. & Thaut, M. H. (2000). *Musical and visual priming of visualization and mental rotation.* Manuscript submitted for publication.

Pearce, J. C. (1992). *Evolution's end.* San Francisco: Harper Collins.

Pelligrini, A. D., & Smith, P. K. (1998a, June). Physical activity play: consensus and debate. *Child Development, 69*(3), 577–598.

Pelligrini, A. D., & Smith, P. K. (1998b, June). Physical activity play: The nature and function of a neglected aspect of play. *Child Development, 69*(3), 609–610.

Persellin, D. (1993, June). Effects of learning modalities on melodic and rhythmic retention on vocal pitch-matching by preschool children. *Perceptual & Motor Skills, 78*(3), Part 2, 1231–1234.

Pert, C. (1997). *Molecules of emotion.* New York: Scribner.

Peterson, C., Maier, S., & Seligman, M. (1993). *Learned helplessness* (pp. 250–255). New York: Oxford University Press.

Petsche, H. (1993). Brain coherence during music activities. *Music Perception, 11,* 117–151.

Pollatschek, J. J., & O'Hagen, F. J. (1989, September). An investigation of the psycho-physical influences of a quality daily physical education program. *Health Education Research.*

Posner, M., & Raichle, M. (1994). *Images of mind* (p. 94). New York: Scientific American Library.

Pratt, R., Abel, H. H., & Skidmore, J. (1995). The effects of neurofeedback training with background music on EEG patterns of ADD and ADHD children. *International Journal of Arts Medicine, 4,* 24–31.

Project Zero. (2000). *The arts and academic improvement: What the evidence shows* (Project REAP—Reviewing Education and the Arts Project). [Online: Executive Summary]. Boston: Project Zero, Graduate School of Education, Harvard University. Available: http://www.pz.harvard.edu/Research/REAP.htm

Ramachandran, V. S., & Hirstein, W. (1999, June/July). The science of art: Art and the brain. *Journal of Consciousness Studies, 6*(6–7), 15–51.

Rauscher, F., Robinson, D., & Jason, J. (1998, July). Improved maze learning through early music exposure in rats. *Neurological Research, 20,* 427–432.

Rauscher, F., Shaw, G., and Ky, K. (1993). Music and spatial task performance. *Nature, 365,* 611.

Rauscher, F., Shaw, G., Levine, L., Wright, E., Dennis, W., & Newcomb, R. (1997). Music training causes long-term development of preschool children's spatial-temporal reasoning. *Neurological Research, 19,* 2–8.

Reber, Arthur. (1993). *Implicit learning and tacit knowledge* (pp. 88–110, 159). New York: Oxford University Press.

Rein, G., & McCraty, R. M. (1995). Effects of positive and negative emotions on salivary IgA. *Journal of Advances in Medicine, 8,* 87–105.

Sallis, J. F., McKenzie, T. L., Alcararaz, J. E., Kolody, B., Faucette, N., & Hovell, M. (1997). The effects of a 2-year physical education program (SPARK) on physical activity and fitness in elementary school students. *American Journal of Public Health, 97,* 1328–1334.

Sallis, J., McKenzie, T., Kolody, B., Lewis, M., Marshall, S., & Rosengard, P. (1999, June). Effects of health-related physical education on academic achievement: Project SPARK. *Research Quarterly for Exercise and Sport, 70*(2), 127.

Samson, S., & Zatorre, R. J. (1994). Contribution of the right temporal lobe to musical timbre discrimination. *Neuropsychologia, 32,* 231–240.

Sarason, S. (1990). *The challenge of art to psychology.* New Haven: Yale University Press.

Sarntheim, J., Petsche, H., Rappelsberger, P., Shaw, G., & von Stein, A. (1998). Synchronization between prefrontal and posterior association cortex during human working memory. *Proceedings of the National Academy of Sciences, USA, 95,* 7092–7096.

Sarntheim, J., von Stein, A., Rappelsberger, P., Petsche, H., Rauscher, F., & Shaw, G. (1997). Persistent patterns of brain activity: An EEG coherence study of the positive effect of music on spatial-temporal reasoning. *Neurological Research, 19,* 107–111.

Sautter, C. (1994, February). An arts education school reform strategy. *Phi Delta Kappan, 2,* 432–436.

Scheel, K. R., & Westefeld, J. S. (1999, Summer). Heavy metal music and adolescent suicidality: An empirical investigation. *Adolescent, 34*(134), 253–273.

Schellenberg, E. G., & Trehub, S. E. (1996). Natural musical intervals: Evidence from infant listeners. *Psychological Science, 7,* 272–277.

Schlaug, G., Jancke, L., Huang, Y., Staiger, J. F., & Steinmetz, H. (1995a). Increased corpus callosum size in musicians. *Neurophysiology, 33,* 1047–1055.

Schlaug, G., Jancke, L., & Pratt, H. (1995b). In vivo evidence of structural brain asymmetry in musicians. *Science, 267,* 699–701.

Seefelt, V., & Vogel, P. (1986). *The value of physical activity.* Reston, VA: American Alliance for Health, Physical Education, Recreation and Dance (AAHPERD) & North American Society of Pacing and Electrophysiology (NASPE). (ERIC Document Reproduction Service No. ED 289 866)

Sergent, J., Zuck, E., Terriah, S., & MacDonald, B. (1992). Distributed neural network underlying musical sight-reading and keyboard performances. *Science, 257,* 106–109.

Shaw, G. (2000). *Keeping Mozart in mind* (p. 31). San Diego: Academic Press.

Shephard, R. (1996). Habitual physical activity and academic performance. *Nutrition Reviews, 54*(4), S32–S35.

Shephard, R. J. (1997). Curricular physical activity and academic performance. *Pediatric Exercise Science, 9,* 113–126.

Silliker, S., & Quirk, J. (1997, March). The effect of extracurricular activity participation on the academic performance of male and female high school students. *The School Counselor, 44,* 288–293.

Silverman, S. (1985). Relationship of engagement and practice trials to student achievement. *Journal of Teaching Physical Education, 5,* 13–21.

Simonds, R., & Scheibel, A. (1989). The postnatal development of the motor speech area: A preliminary study. *Brain and Language, 37,* 41–58.

Sitting down on the job: Not as easy as it sounds (1981, October). *Occupational Health and Safety, 50*(10), 24–26.

Sousou, S. D. (1997, August). Effects of melody and lyric on mood and memory. *Perceptual Motor Skills, 85*(1), 31–40.

Spitzer, M. (1999). *The mind within the net.* Cambridge, MA: MIT Press.

Stein, B., Hardy, C. A., & Totten, H. (1984). The use of music and imagery to enhance and accelerate information retention. *Journal of the Society for Accelerative Learning & Teaching, 7*(4).

Stevenson, H. W., & Lee, S. Y. (1990). Contexts of achievement. *Monographs of the Society for Research in Child Development, 55*(1–2, Serial no. 221).

Stiggins, R. (1993). *In teachers' hands: Investigating the practice of classroom assessment.* Albany: State University of New York (SUNY).

Stratton, V. N., & Zalanowski, A. H. (1995). The effects of music and paintings on mood. *Journal of Music Therapy, 26,* 30–41.

Sutter, M. L., & Schreiner, C. E. (1991). Physiology and topography of neurons with multipeaked tuning curves in cat primary auditory cortex. *Journal of Neurophysiology, 65,* 1207–1226.

Swartz, D. W., & Tomlinson, R. W. (1990). Spectral response patterns of auditory cortex neurons to harmonic complex tones in alert monkeys. *Journal of Neurophysiology, 64*(1), 282–298.

Terr, L. (1999). *Beyond love and work: Why adults need to play* (pp. 30–31). New York: Scribner Books, Simon & Schuster.

Terry, S. (1998, September). Genius at work. *Fast Company Magazine, 17,* 170.

Terwogt, M. M., & VanGrinsven, F. (1988). Recognition of emotions in music by children and adults. *Perceptual and Motor Skills, 67,* 697–698.

Thaut, M., Schleiffers, S., & Davis, W. (1991). Analysis of EMG activity in biceps and triceps muscle in an upper extremity gross motor task under the influence of auditory rhythm. *Journal of Music Therapy, 28,* 64–68.

Thayer, R. (1996). *The origin of everyday moods* (pp. 128–132). New York: Oxford University Press.

Thompson, B. M., & Andrews, S. R. (1999). The emerging field of sound training. *IEEE Engineering in Medicine and Biology Magazine, 3–4,* 99.

Tittle, H., & Webber, M. (1973). Dilemmas in a general theory of planning. *Policy Science, 4,* 155–169.

Tomatis, A. (1996). *The ear and language.* Norval, ON, Canada: Mouling Publishing.

Tomporowski, P., & Ellis, N. (1986). Effects of exercise on cognitive processes: A review. *Psychological Bulletin, 99*(3), 338–346.

Took, K. J., & Weiss, D. (1994). Heavy metal, rap and adolescent behavior. *Adolescence, 29,* 613–621.

Tranel, D., & Damasio, A. R. (1985). Knowledge without awareness. *Science, 228,* 1453–1454.

Travlos, A., & Marisi, D. (1995). Information processing and concentration as a function of fitness level and exercise-induced activation in exhaustion. *Perceptual & Motor Skills, 89*(1), 15–26, 248.

Trehub, S. E., Bull, D., & Thorpe, L. A. (1984, June). Infant's perception of melodies: The role of melodic contour. *Child Development, 55*(3), 821–830.

Trehub, S. E., & Thorpe, L. A. (1989). Infant's perception of rhythm: Categorization of auditory sequences by temporal structure. *Canadian Journal of Psychology, 43,* 217–229.

U.S. Department of Health and Human Services. (1996). *Physical activity and health: A report of the Surgeon General.* [Online report]. Atlanta, GA: U.S. Department of Health and Human Services, Centers for Disease Control and Prevention, National Center for Chronic Disease Prevention and Health Promotion, and President's Council on Physical Fitness and Sports. Available: http://www.cdc.gov/nccdphp/sgr/pdf/sgrfull.pdf

U.S. Department of Health and Human Services. (1999). *Promoting better health for young people through physical activity and sports: A report to the President from the Secretary of Health and Human Services and the Secretary of Education.* [Online report]. Atlanta, GA: U.S. Department of Health and Human Services, Centers for Disease Control and Prevention, National Center for Chronic Disease Prevention and Health Promotion, Office of the Secretary, Office of Public Health and Science, President's Council on Physical Fitness and Sports, and U.S. Department of Education. Available: http://www.cdc.gov/nccdphp/dash/presphysactrpt/index.htm

VanderArk, S., & Ely, D. (1992). Biochemical and galvanic skin responses to music stimuli by college students in biology and music. *Perceptual and Motor Skills, 74,* 1079–1090.

van Praag, H., Kempermann, G., & Gage, F. (1999, March). Running increases cell proliferation in the adult mouse dentate gyrus. *Nature Neuroscience, 2*(3), 266–270.

Wagner, M. (1997, February). The effects of isotonic resistance exercise on aggressive variable in adult male inmates in the Texas Dept. of Criminal Justice. (Texas A&M Univ.: UMI Order #AAM9701731). *Dissertation Abstracts International, Sect. A: Humanities & Social Sciences, 57*(8A), 3442.

Wallin, N., Merker, B., & Brown, S. (1999). *The origins of music. A Bradford book.* Cambridge, MA: MIT Press.

Walling, D. (2000). *Rethinking how art is taught.* Thousand Oaks, CA: Corwin Press.

Weinberger, N. (1998). Creating creativity with music. *Musica Research Notes, 5*(2), 2.

Weinberger, N., & McKenna, T. M. (1988). Sensitivity of single neurons in auditory cortex to contour: Toward a neurophysiology of music perception. *Music Perception, 5,* 355–390.

Wiggin, R. G. (1962). Teaching mentally handicapped children through art. *Art Education Bulletin, 19*(5), 20–24.

Wiggins, G. P. (1993). *Assessing student performance: Exploring the purpose and limits of testing.* San Francisco: Jossey-Bass.

Wilson, F. (1999). *Hand: How its use shapes the brain, language, and human culture.* New York: Vintage Books.

Wilson, M. A., & McNaughton, B. L. (1994). Reactivation of hippocampal ensemble memories during sleep. *Science, 265,* 676–679.

Wingert, M. (1972). Effects of a music enrichment program in the education of the mentally retarded. *Journal of Music Therapy, 9*(1), 13–22.

Winter, M. J., Paskin, S., & Baker, T. (1994). Music reduces stress and anxiety of patients in the surgical holding area. *Journal of Post Anesthesia Nursing, 9,* 340–343.

Wisconsin Department of Public Instruction. (1997, June). *Wisconsin's model academic standards for arts.* Milwaukee, WI: Author. Available as separate booklets for art education, drama, visual arts, dance, and music from Publications, WI Dept. of Public Instruction, Drawer 179, Milwaukee, WI 53293-0179, or on the Web (http://www.dpi.state.wi.us/dpi/dltcl/eis/pubsales/arts.html).

Wolf, D. P., & Pistone, N. (1991). *Taking full measure: Rethinking assessment through the arts.* (Locator #NX 282 W6). New York: College Entrance Examination Board.

Wolff, K. L. (1979). The effects of general music education on the academic achievement, perceptual-motor development, creative thinking and school attendance of first graders. *Dissertation Abstracts International, 40,* 5359A.

Zacharkow, D. (1988). *Posture: Sitting, standing, chair design and exercise* (pp. 101–112). Springfield, IL: Charles C Thomas.

Zatorre, R., Evans, A., & Meyer, E. (1994). Neural mechanisms underlying melodic perception and memory for pitch. *Journal of Neuroscience, 14*(4), 1908–1919.

Zeki, S. (1993). *A vision of the brain.* Oxford, UK: Blackwell Scientific Publications.

Zeki, S. (1999). Art and the brain. *Journal of Consciousness Studies, 6*(6–7), 76–95.

Index

About the Author

Eric Jensen's passion is the brain and learning. He has taught at the elementary, middle school, and senior high school levels, as well as at three California universities. In 1981, he co-founded SuperCamp, the most successful brain-compatible learning program for students in the United States; the camp has more than 35,000 graduates. He helped introduce brain-based learning to four continents. Jensen authored the best-selling ASCD book, *Teaching with the Brain in Mind,* as well as *Student Success Secrets, SuperTeaching, The Learning Brain, Brain-Based Learning,* and eight other books. He's spoken at most major conferences, and his work has been featured in *USA Today,* in *The Wall Street Journal,* and on CNN. Jensen is a staff developer and member of the Society for Neuroscience and the New York Academy of Science. Eric Jensen speaks at conferences on the arts and Teaching with the Brain in Mind.

Jensen also provides in-depth educational opportunities, such as the following:

· *6-Day Workshop:"Teaching with the Brain in Mind"* focuses on what we know about how the brain works and how to apply practical strategies to learning, memory and student performance.

· *5-Day Facilitator Training: "Presenting with the Brain in Mind"* applies what we know about the brain and learning to front of the room presentation skills.

· *3-Day "Fragile Brain" Program: "Different Brains, Different Learners"* presents cutting-edge knowledge on dyslexia, attention deficit, helplessness, depression, drug abuse, anxiety, learning disabilities, and other challenges to help you reach the hard-to-reach learners.

Author contact: Eric Jensen, Box 2551, Del Mar, CA 92014; Phone: (858) 642-0400; E-mail: eric@jlcbrain.com; Fax: (858) 642-0404

Related ASCD Resources: Arts and the Brain

Audiotapes

Achieving Major Goals with Brain-Based Learning, by Joan Caulfield and Wayne Jennings (#200173)

Designing Performance-Based Teaching and Learning, Part I (set of 3 tapes), by Heidi Hayes Jacobs, Grant Wiggins, Robert Marzano, and Debra Pickering (#295040)

Exploring the Child Development Insights Provided by Brain Research, by Maria Almandare Barron (#298139)

Emotion/Attention: Our Brain's Doorway to Reason and Logic, by Robert Sylwester, (#200114)

A Healthy Brain in the Learning Process, by Deborah G. Estes (#200156)

How Can Educators Use Knowledge About the Human Brain to Improve School Learning? by Eric Jensen, Renate Nummela Caine, and Robert Sylwester (#200096)

CD-ROM and Multimedia

Exploring Our Multiple Intelligences CD-ROM, (#596276)

The Human Brain Professional Inquiry Kit, by Bonnie Benesh (#99900)

Online Resources

Visit ASCD's Web site (www.ascd.org) for the following professional development opportunities:

Online Tutorials: *The Brain and Learning; Performance Assessments* (http://www.ascd.org/frametutorials.html)

Professional Development Online: *The Brain* (http://www.ascd.org/framepdonline.html) (for a small fee; password protected)

Print Products

Activating and Engaging Habits of Mind, by Art Costa and Bena Kallick (#100033)

ASCD Topic Pack: *Brain-Based Learning Topic Pack* (#197194)

A Celebration of Neurons: An Educator's Guide to the Human Brain by Robert Sylwester (#195085)

Dimensions of Learning Teachers' Manual, 2nd Edition (#197133) by Robert J. Marzano, Debra Pickering, and others

A Field Guide to Using Visual Tools, by David Hyerle (#100023)

Learning and Memory: The Brain in Action, by Marilee Sprenger (#199213)

Powerful Learning, by Ron Brandt (#198179)

Teaching with the Brain in Mind, by Eric Jensen (#198019)

Understanding by Design (#198199) by Grant Wiggins and Jay McTighe

Unleashing the Power of Perceptual Change: The Potential of Brain-Based Teaching, by Renate Nummela Caine and Geoffrey Caine, (#197170)

Visual Tools for Constructing Knowledge (#196072) by David Hyerle.

Videotapes

The Brain and Early Childhood (two tapes, #400054).

The Brain and Learning (four tapes, #498062).

The Brain and Mathematics Series (two tapes, #400237)

The Brain and Reading (three tapes, #499207).

How to Use Graphic Organizers to Promote Student Thinking (#499048), Tape 6 of the "How To" Series.

Concept Definition Map (#499262), Tape 5 of The Lesson Collection Video Series: Reading Strategies.

For additional information, visit us on the World Wide Web (http://www.ascd.org), send an e-mail message to member@ascd.org, call the ASCD Service Center (1-800-933-ASCD or 703-578-9600, then press 2), send a fax to 703-575-5400, or write to Information Services, ASCD, 1703 N. Beauregard St., Alexandria, VA 22311-1714 USA.